CARD MAGIC

First published in 2008 by New Holland Publishers (UK) Ltd
London • Cape Town • Sydney • Auckland

1 3 5 7 9 10 8 6 4 2

www.newhollandpublishers.com

Garfield House, 86–88 Edgware Road, London W2 2EA, UK

80 McKenzie Street, Cape Town 8001, South Africa

Unit 1, 66 Gibbes Street, Chatswood, NSW 2067, Australia

218 Lake Road, Northcote, Auckland, New Zealand

ISBN 978 184773 329 0

Publishing Director: Rosemary Wilkinson
Publisher: Aruna Vasudevan
Editors: Steffanie Brown, Julia Shone
Artworks: Steve Crisp
Design and cover design: Ian Hughes, Mousemat Design Ltd
Production: Melanie Dowland

Printed and bound in China by Leo Paper Group

*Note: The author and publishers have made every effort to ensure that the information given in this
book is accurate, but they cannot accept liability for any resulting loss or damage to either property or
person, whether direct or consequential and howsoever arising.*

MARC LEMEZMA'S
CARD
MAGIC

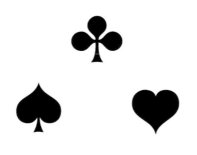

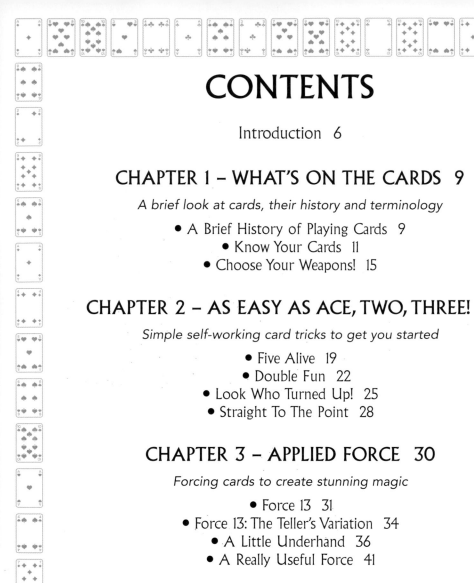

CONTENTS

Introduction 6

CHAPTER 1 – WHAT'S ON THE CARDS 9

A brief look at cards, their history and terminology

CHAPTER 2 – AS EASY AS ACE, TWO, THREE! 18

Simple self-working card tricks to get you started

CHAPTER 3 – APPLIED FORCE 30

Forcing cards to create stunning magic

CHAPTER 4 – IT ALL ADDS UP TO MAGIC 43

Amazing card magic using maths and numbers

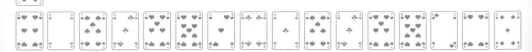

CHAPTER 5 – 'SLEIGHTLY TRICKIER' 57

A selection of miracles using real card technique and sleight of hand

CHAPTER 6 – IT'S ALL MADE UP 71

A collection of card and packet tricks magic using made-up cards

CHAPTER 7 – KILLER 'KARDS' 85

A final selection of powerful card magic with which to close

INTRODUCTION

I hope you're ready for this…
…because I am going to make your fingers hurt!

Old friends turn up at the most unexpected times, and for many of us, playing cards are indeed 'old friends'. We may be hunting through our drawers, seeking an old picture or passport, and chance upon a worn packet of cards that we haven't seen for what seems like years. We gaze wistfully at them, recalling happy times with our families and friends, playing games around the fire on a cold winter's afternoon. Even though the cards are worn and dirty, they hold a unique place in our hearts and minds.

Not all of us see cards in such a positive light, however. For some people they have a strong association with inappropriate pursuits such as gambling, sorcery (supposedly the bad kind of magic!), sin and even the work of Beelzebub himself – some people even refer to a deck of playing cards as 'The Devil's Picture-book'!

If you are one of those persons who, for religious or cultural reasons, dislikes or is not allowed to use or even touch playing cards, then this book is quite obviously not for you. If, however, you are keen to learn some great magic tricks with cards and how to perform them sensibly, then I think you have made a great decision in purchasing this book.

MY LIFE WITH CARDS

My fascination with cards and card tricks started over 40 years ago. One of the first magic tricks I learned as an eager 6-year-old was a card trick that was taught to me by my father. It was a simple trick that worked itself, and was thus an ideal way for me to learn how to 'do magic'. Over the years I progressed, learning some more complex tricks and practising my sleight of hand until my fingers hurt. I acquired hundreds of pamphlets, books and videos and learned how thousands of tricks

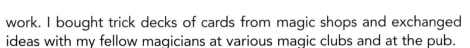

work. I bought trick decks of cards from magic shops and exchanged ideas with my fellow magicians at various magic clubs and at the pub.

No matter how proficient I became with cards, I was always in awe of the technical skills of some of my friends who, even though I knew what they were doing, performed their tricks so elegantly.

Eventually magic became my life, and I quit my 'real job' in computing and started performing for a living. With all those thousands of card tricks in my repertoire surely I had an unbeatable arsenal of sleight of hand miracles with which to bombard my audience!

Most magicians know more card tricks than all the other kinds of tricks they perform combined, and I am, most certainly, no exception. Yet despite the myriad of magic I know how to do, I actually only perform 20 or so card tricks on a regular basis. The same is typically true for any professional magician; we know thousands of different illusions, yet we choose to learn how to do a small selection of tricks really well. This allows us to amaze our audience without boring them, and to hopefully leave them wanting more.

I hope this book gives you an enticing list of recipes with which you can experiment and eventually serve up a tasty, balanced menu of magic for your audience!

... AND SO THIS BOOK

You might assume that being a professional magician I will only use the most complex techniques when performing. In reality, I use a complete mixture of sleight of hand, mechanisms, psychology and even tricks that work themselves. The real secret to success is using the right trick (with the right method) at the right time for the right effect!

You might find it interesting to know that my favourite card trick is one that works itself. I do nothing other than lay out the cards in a certain way and tell a story. This one piece of magic gets the most incredible reactions, but I need to be careful about when and where to use it. (Of course, I do other tricks with many technical moves and they get a great response too.)

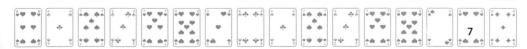

This is a good lesson for us all as it shows that there is not always a correlation between the degree of sleight of hand that you use and the impact a trick will have on your audience. Be it with cards, coins or rabbits, the effect our magic has on our audience is more about us as people than it is about the raw method we use to achieve the effect.

We need to cover a lot of bases in this book, but I hope it will give you, whether you are a complete novice or are already performing tricks, a good grounding in the basics and principles of card magic.

First of all, we will look at the history of cards and get to know some of the terminology surrounding card tricks. Then our journey will take us through some simple tricks, after which we will add some sleights of hand and various moves, building up to some incredible tricks for our finale.

If you have read any of my previous books – in particular, *Mind Magic* (New Holland, 2003) and *Mind Tricks* (New Holland, 2007) – you will know that I like to weave intriguing stories into my books. In this book there will be a little less of this, primarily because there will be more techniques to describe in the limited space we have.

I have, however, added a new idea to this book. There are so many subtleties, nuances and bold secrets that we can learn from every trick, and these can add value to the rest of our magic. So, at the end of each trick I will highlight one or two points or principles that are worthy of our attention in that they can be applied to other tricks in this book or elsewhere.

But the important thing, as I always seem to say in my books, is for you to read about the ideas and then play with them. Discard what you do not like and work hard on those elements that appeal. This way, you can make the magic your own – and that is the most magical and powerful thing you can ever do.

Read on and enjoy!

CHAPTER 1
WHAT'S ON THE CARDS?

As he enters his trade, every apprentice must learn the basic rules and terminology of his chosen craft. As he progresses, he will gain a deeper understanding of his tools and raw materials. Eventually, he will have developed his skills to the point where he can fairly and squarely be called a master of his trade.

The purpose of this chapter is to introduce you to your deck of cards so that you know a little about their origins and the common terminology associated with them. Providing you with an accurate history of playing cards is, however, somewhat of a challenge. Here in the United Kingdom we tend to have a narrow view of how playing cards look and what they represent; this view is influenced by our knowledge of Anglo-American history and culture.

In the past many cultures played games using stones, coins and seeds as tokens. Over time these games became more complex, and different values were assigned to the playing pieces. Nowadays, practically every culture has some form of gaming piece or token that reflects its own history and has its own artistic influences. So who actually invented playing cards?

A BRIEF HISTORY OF PLAYING CARDS

It is generally agreed that the roots of modern playing cards lie in ancient China, where a system of paper currency evolved during the 9th and 10th centuries. In some ways this system can be seen as a forerunner to both modern banknotes and playing cards, as not only did they have different denominations, they also had different groups, or suits. The lowest value note in this ancient Chinese system depicted a single coin, for example, while other notes in the same 'suit' had various numbers of coins. The next suit represented strings of coins (our ancient friends carried coins on strings rather than in purses, which is why the coins had holes in the middle), while other suits involved multiple strings, and so on. Of course, everyone likes a wager, and many games of luck and chance would have been played for money using these notes. Thus, from this single root we can see links to currency, playing cards, dominoes and other tokens of value throughout history.

But this is just one theory of the origins of playing cards; a quick search on the internet would probably lead you to dozens of different versions. For example, another theory postulates that playing cards developed from Tarot cards. Many disagree with this view, however the fact that the playing cards used in Italy and southern Europe actually have the same suits as Tarot cards is a persuasive argument in favour of this theory. To make matters even more confusing, around the 13th century another system of cards, this time originating from the Islamic world, came to Europe. These cards used a four-suit system, not unlike the one we use today.

The origins of the court cards (Jack, Queen, King) are even less clear. Some say they were first seen in the Islamic system of cards, while others suggest they were an attempt to have permanent Trump, or *Triomphe* cards in the deck. We do know for certain, however, that playing cards reflected the social situations in which they were created and the games people chose to play with them. In this way, court cards were decorated with caricatures of royalty and politicians, often parodying scandals of the time. For example, the Queen of Hearts in the traditional English deck is meant to represent Elizabeth of York (1466–1503), who was Consort to King Henry VII (1457–1509; reigned 1485–1509). This concept of playing cards reflecting political realities can be seen more recently in the 'Most Wanted' decks. These show the faces of the leaders of the Iraqi regime and were distributed by the United States government to the allied forces during the second Gulf War. A quick look through various card catalogues shows many decks with all manner of social and political satire in their designs.

In the last two centuries, the 52-card deck with which we are familiar here in the United Kingdom has become standard in most parts of the Western world, especially for those who play Bridge and Poker. In fact, this deck system has now influenced that in southern Europe, where a Queen has now been added to each suit (previously all three picture or court cards were male)

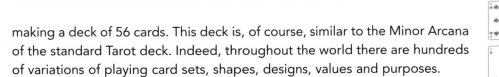

making a deck of 56 cards. This deck is, of course, similar to the Minor Arcana of the standard Tarot deck. Indeed, throughout the world there are hundreds of variations of playing card sets, shapes, designs, values and purposes.

KNOW YOUR CARDS

In the Anglo-American world of magic the 52-card (plus Joker) deck seems to be the norm, and that is what the tricks described in this book are based upon. Of course the choice of which cards you use is your own, but there are several factors in favour of using this deck whilst performing magic in the Western world. Generally speaking, Western cards are seen as standard tools of the magician's trade. Furthermore, there is a movement in modern magic towards props appearing 'normal' to the audience, and thus it would seem only logical to use cards from one's own culture. Then there is the choice of material. There is a huge wealth of card tricks written up in books like this one, and an immense array of card tricks available from magic dealers. Most of these use the Western deck of cards, and so it might seem churlish not to use the same deck. (That said, most of the tricks in this book could be adapted to almost any form of cards with some thought and a little application.)

My suggestion to you is that you should observe what happens in magic shows in your part of the world. Which types of deck do other magicians in your area use? You can then decide whether you wish to conform to this practice, or whether you wish to create a unique style all your own.

Below is a collection of useful terms related to playing cards that we will be using throughout this book. I have decided to put this section at the beginning of the book because you will need to know the definitions of these words as you progress through the tricks. You will most likely already know the meaning of some of these terms, but please read through them anyway. You never know, you might learn something new!

Deck – a full set of playing cards. The number in the set is, of course, dependent upon the type and origins of the deck. This term is interchangeable with the word PACK, although technically a pack of cards is *in* its box while a deck refers to cards that are *out* of the box.

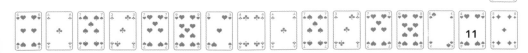

Case – the box our cards live in.

Card – the singular part of a deck of cards. In some decks the cards are all unique, while in others there are duplicates. In any case, each card has a number of elements.

Face – the side of the card that shows the number, suit and value that make that card unique.

Spot Card – in a Western deck the cards numbered Ace through ten are so called because the number of spots printed on them indicates their value.

Picture Card – in a Western deck the cards that depict the Jack, Queen and King. These cards are also known as court cards (derived from the royal courts). Also referred to as Trump (from the French *Triomphe*) cards.

Value – the numerical or Trump value of a card. For example, cards Ace (or one) to ten assume this numerical value. The Jack, Queen and King may also be given the values of 11, 12 and 13 respectively.

Ace – the card with the value of 1, although sometimes it has a value of 10 in card games. Typically the most important or highest ranking card in each suit.

Suit – the groups to which cards of different values belong. In our Western deck we have four suits: Clubs, Hearts, Diamonds and Spades. The shapes of the spots on each card indicate the suits.

Index – the number and spot usually found in the top left- and bottom right-hand corners of each card, showing the value and suit of that card. Some cards have an index in all four corners, while other cards (particularly older decks) have no indices at all.

Back – the side of a card that is typically the same on all the cards in a deck; usually decorated with a geometric design that is unique to each brand of cards. Sometimes there may be other artwork or advertising on the backs of the cards.

Top of the Deck – in a deck that is arranged normally (i.e. faces and backs all facing the same way), this refers to the card at the upper extremity of the deck that sits with its back facing you.

Bottom of the Deck – in a deck that is arranged normally, this refers to the card at the lower extremity of the deck that sits with its face downwards. This term is more or less synonymous with Face of the Deck (*see below*).

Face of the Deck – refers to the card at the bottom of the deck whose face is showing. This term is more or less synonymous with Bottom of the Deck (*see above*).

Stock – a group of cards in a deck that stay together (perhaps because they are pre-arranged). We sometimes refer to a top, middle or bottom stock.

Packet – a group of cards on their own (outside of a deck). A magician may have different packets of cards on his table during a trick.

Box – this term actually has two definitions. One is, of course, the box that the cards come in. But we also refer to cards as being 'boxed' when one or more cards in a deck are facing around the wrong way, i.e. lying face to face or back to back.

Stack – a packet, stock or deck of cards that is in a special pre-arranged order (usually unknown to your audience).

Face Down – a card, packet, stock, stack or deck that is lying with the faces of the cards downward (on your table, or perhaps in your hand) and with the backs facing upwards.

Face Up – a card, packet, stock, stack or deck that is lying with the faces of the cards upward and with the backs downwards.

Spread – this term has two closely related meanings. One is to 'spread' the cards in a line on a table, while the other involves running the cards from one hand to the other, pushing with the thumb, typically to display them or to have one selected.

Fan – to spread the cards so as to form a circular shape. This is sometimes done in order to have cards chosen, but more often as a showy flourish.

Square – to square the cards or deck is to bring them all neatly into a line.

Deal – to lay the cards on the table, one at a time, taking them in turn from the top of the deck.

Shuffle – to alter or mix the order of a packet or deck of cards.

Overhand Shuffle – the standard shuffle whereby the cards are held vertically in the left hand whilst the right hand removes random packets and places them back in different locations.

Hindu Shuffle – popular in Asia and used by magicians worldwide, in this shuffle the cards are held horizontally in the left hand and packets are drawn out with the right and replaced randomly.

Riffle – to flick through the pack with, for example, your thumb.

Riffle Shuffle – where the deck is split into two halves and the ends are meshed together by riffling the thumb down the edges.

False Shuffle – to 'seem to' mix the order of a packet or deck of cards, yet retain their original order. Sometimes only a single card, packet or stock of cards is kept in order, or are put into a specific position by a false shuffle.

Cut – to lift a random stock of cards from the top of the deck and place it to one side.

Complete the Cut – to place the remaining stock of cards left by our cut, on top of the stock we cut off, thus randomizing the deck.

False Cut – a cut that does not change the arrangement of the deck, or that leaves specific cards or stocks of cards in a particular position. This manoeuvre is, of course, unknown to the audience.

Self Working – a card trick (or any magic trick) that 'works itself' requiring no significant technical skill or dexterity on the part of the magician.

Force – to ask your helper (during a magic trick) to choose a specific card, or to choose from a narrow selection of cards, whilst apparently giving them a choice of all 52!

Sleight of Hand – a secret or hidden move or action that enables the magician to make his 'magic' happen.

Flourish – a fancy move or display made using the cards in order to show your skill.

Colour Change – a move whereby you visibly change one card for another.

Palm – to secretly hold a card (or any object) in one's hand so that the audience is unaware of its presence.

Break – to secretly hold a gap between cards, stocks or stacks within a deck so that we can quickly locate and move the cards we need by feel alone.

Jog – to secretly position a card or stock of cards within a deck so that they lie offset from the rest, thus making it easy for us to locate the point at which one stock ends and the other begins. This enables us to easily move whole stocks around to where we need them. Cards may be out-jogged or in-jogged.

Gimmicked – a card, stack, packet, stock or even a whole deck that has been physically modified (for example, cut short) in order to assist with a magic

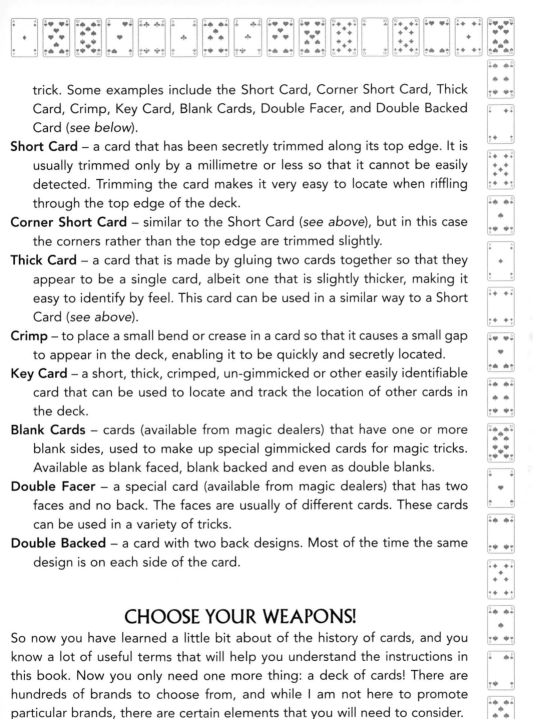

trick. Some examples include the Short Card, Corner Short Card, Thick Card, Crimp, Key Card, Blank Cards, Double Facer, and Double Backed Card (*see below*).

Short Card – a card that has been secretly trimmed along its top edge. It is usually trimmed only by a millimetre or less so that it cannot be easily detected. Trimming the card makes it very easy to locate when riffling through the top edge of the deck.

Corner Short Card – similar to the Short Card (*see above*), but in this case the corners rather than the top edge are trimmed slightly.

Thick Card – a card that is made by gluing two cards together so that they appear to be a single card, albeit one that is slightly thicker, making it easy to identify by feel. This card can be used in a similar way to a Short Card (*see above*).

Crimp – to place a small bend or crease in a card so that it causes a small gap to appear in the deck, enabling it to be quickly and secretly located.

Key Card – a short, thick, crimped, un-gimmicked or other easily identifiable card that can be used to locate and track the location of other cards in the deck.

Blank Cards – cards (available from magic dealers) that have one or more blank sides, used to make up special gimmicked cards for magic tricks. Available as blank faced, blank backed and even as double blanks.

Double Facer – a special card (available from magic dealers) that has two faces and no back. The faces are usually of different cards. These cards can be used in a variety of tricks.

Double Backed – a card with two back designs. Most of the time the same design is on each side of the card.

CHOOSE YOUR WEAPONS!

So now you have learned a little bit about of the history of cards, and you know a lot of useful terms that will help you understand the instructions in this book. Now you only need one more thing: a deck of cards! There are hundreds of brands to choose from, and while I am not here to promote particular brands, there are certain elements that you will need to consider.

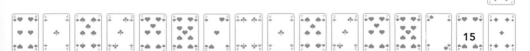

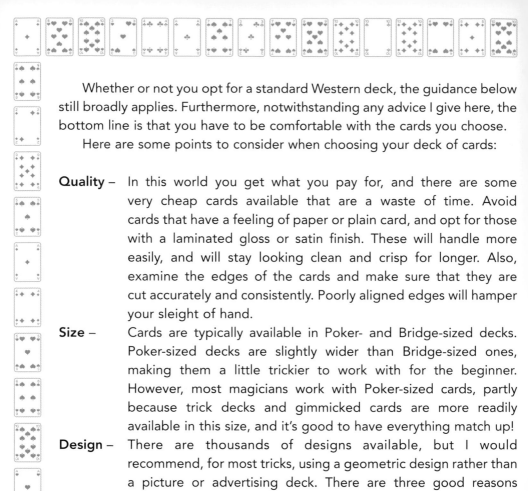

Whether or not you opt for a standard Western deck, the guidance below still broadly applies. Furthermore, notwithstanding any advice I give here, the bottom line is that you have to be comfortable with the cards you choose.

Here are some points to consider when choosing your deck of cards:

Quality – In this world you get what you pay for, and there are some very cheap cards available that are a waste of time. Avoid cards that have a feeling of paper or plain card, and opt for those with a laminated gloss or satin finish. These will handle more easily, and will stay looking clean and crisp for longer. Also, examine the edges of the cards and make sure that they are cut accurately and consistently. Poorly aligned edges will hamper your sleight of hand.

Size – Cards are typically available in Poker- and Bridge-sized decks. Poker-sized decks are slightly wider than Bridge-sized ones, making them a little trickier to work with for the beginner. However, most magicians work with Poker-sized cards, partly because trick decks and gimmicked cards are more readily available in this size, and it's good to have everything match up!

Design – There are thousands of designs available, but I would recommend, for most tricks, using a geometric design rather than a picture or advertising deck. There are three good reasons for this. Firstly, we don't want the pictures to become the star of the show. Also, the geometry more readily hides gimmicks and cuts and can also mask the odd sleight. Perhaps most importantly, some geometric designs have matching gimmicks readily available.

One thing I would totally avoid is a deck with nudity or other images of dubious taste. You might like them, but it would be unfair to foist them onto your audience. I suggest going to a toy or games shop, or perhaps even a drug store, and buying a few different decks. Experiment until you find a design you like and stick with it. If you can find a magic dealer, even better – you will have a huge choice from which to make your selection.

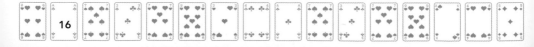

If pushed, I would suggest Piatnik cards from Austria, or Bicycle cards from the United States. Both are good quality and both have a fantastic range of extra cards and gimmicks readily available. Once you have made a choice, buy a few decks, getting a mix of blue and red backs (as you'll need them for some of the tricks), and you're ready to learn your first piece of Card Magic!

CHAPTER 2
AS EASY AS ACE, TWO, THREE!

I have always believed that the best way to do anything of which you are nervous or scared is to just do it! Once you have broken the ice and gained a feel for what you are doing, you can then begin to learn and develop even greater skills. Later in this book we will learn some quite complex card tricks, which in some cases use sleight of hand. The techniques and moves you will need for these tricks will take some time to practise, so to help you on your way this chapter will show you a small selection of tricks that are essentially self-working. Many keen amateur magicians and magic 'enthusiasts' are quite snobbish about using self-working tricks, but you will find that almost every professional working magician uses some such material in their act. If it is a good trick that suits your style, then why leave it on the shelf? Of course, the term 'self-working' is a misnomer, as all magic tricks, no matter how easy the method, need to be 'worked'. That means that the performer (you!) needs to present the effect with confidence and clarity.

For example, some tricks rely upon your spectators following specific instructions. If you seem uncertain or unclear about what they are to do and you hesitate or equivocate, they will soon realise that the order of events is crucial to the effect and will easily spot your method. If you can deliver your tricks with confidence, however, the importance of each stage will become lost in the flow and anticipation of real magic.

In this chapter there are four simple but effective tricks to get you started. My advice is to choose one of these four tricks – the one that appeals to you most – and learn and practise it until you are really

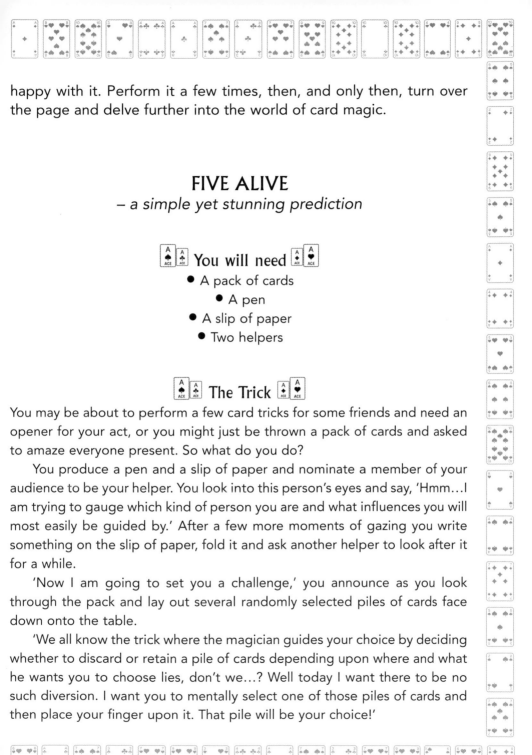

happy with it. Perform it a few times, then, and only then, turn over the page and delve further into the world of card magic.

FIVE ALIVE
– a simple yet stunning prediction

You will need
- A pack of cards
- A pen
- A slip of paper
- Two helpers

The Trick

You may be about to perform a few card tricks for some friends and need an opener for your act, or you might just be thrown a pack of cards and asked to amaze everyone present. So what do you do?

You produce a pen and a slip of paper and nominate a member of your audience to be your helper. You look into this person's eyes and say, 'Hmm…I am trying to gauge which kind of person you are and what influences you will most easily be guided by.' After a few more moments of gazing you write something on the slip of paper, fold it and ask another helper to look after it for a while.

'Now I am going to set you a challenge,' you announce as you look through the pack and lay out several randomly selected piles of cards face down onto the table.

'We all know the trick where the magician guides your choice by deciding whether to discard or retain a pile of cards depending upon where and what he wants you to choose lies, don't we…? Well today I want there to be no such diversion. I want you to mentally select one of those piles of cards and then place your finger upon it. That pile will be your choice!'

Your helper ponders for a moment and puts his finger on one of the piles. You ask the person holding the slip of paper to open it out and read your prediction aloud. It reads: From all the random piles of cards, I know you will choose the FIVE pile.

You turn over the remaining piles and they are indeed made up of random cards, but when you turn over the chosen pile it is comprised of the four fives!

The Secret

The secret to this trick is deceptively simple. EVERY pile is a five pile. Here's what you need to do.

Write your prediction as above and hand it to your helper for safekeeping, then sort through the cards and lay out five piles, running from left to right. We'll name them Piles A to E for clarity.

Pile A (on your left) contains a random number of cards (say eight or nine).
Pile B contains five cards.
Pile C contains an ACE and two TWOs.
Pile D contains four FIVES.
Pile E (on your right) contains a random number, say ten or more.
Think about it. With this set-up, any one of the piles can be described as the FIVE pile! Here's how:

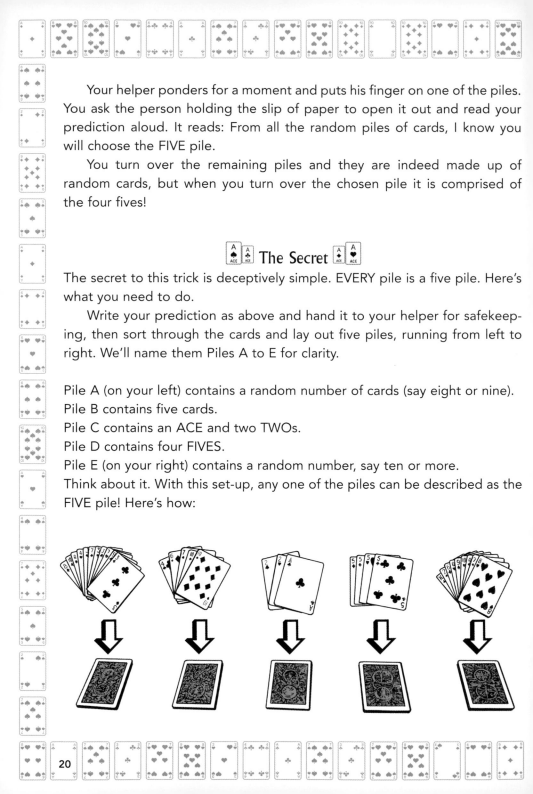

20

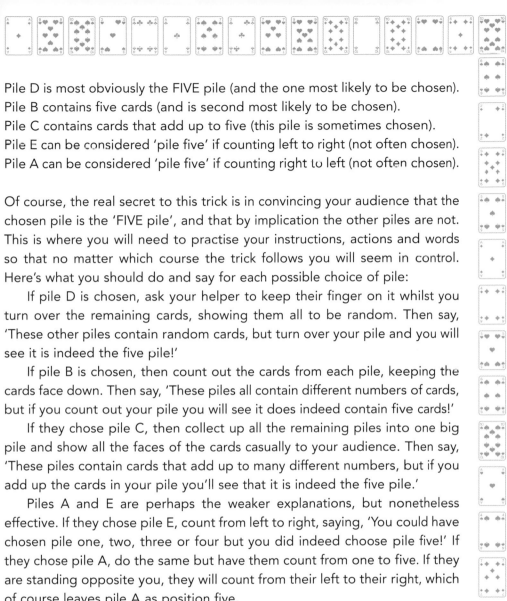

Pile D is most obviously the FIVE pile (and the one most likely to be chosen).
Pile B contains five cards (and is second most likely to be chosen).
Pile C contains cards that add up to five (this pile is sometimes chosen).
Pile E can be considered 'pile five' if counting left to right (not often chosen).
Pile A can be considered 'pile five' if counting right to left (not often chosen).

Of course, the real secret to this trick is in convincing your audience that the chosen pile is the 'FIVE pile', and that by implication the other piles are not. This is where you will need to practise your instructions, actions and words so that no matter which course the trick follows you will seem in control. Here's what you should do and say for each possible choice of pile:

If pile D is chosen, ask your helper to keep their finger on it whilst you turn over the remaining cards, showing them all to be random. Then say, 'These other piles contain random cards, but turn over your pile and you will see it is indeed the five pile!'

If pile B is chosen, then count out the cards from each pile, keeping the cards face down. Then say, 'These piles all contain different numbers of cards, but if you count out your pile you will see it does indeed contain five cards!'

If they chose pile C, then collect up all the remaining piles into one big pile and show all the faces of the cards casually to your audience. Then say, 'These piles contain cards that add up to many different numbers, but if you add up the cards in your pile you'll see that it is indeed the five pile.'

Piles A and E are perhaps the weaker explanations, but nonetheless effective. If they chose pile E, count from left to right, saying, 'You could have chosen pile one, two, three or four but you did indeed choose pile five!' If they chose pile A, do the same but have them count from one to five. If they are standing opposite you, they will count from their left to their right, which of course leaves pile A as position five.

🂡 Final Thoughts 🂡

I first read about the principle of this trick in a book I have had since I was a child. This version is adapted to consider the relative probabilities of each pile being chosen so that the most convincing outcome will occur more frequently.

The key to performing this trick is confidence in delivering your final line. Make good use of the word 'indeed'. You might also want to consider moving on to another card trick fairly quickly so that the audience has no time to dwell on what has just happened.

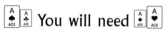 What Have We Learned?

That which goes unseen or unsaid in magic is often more effective than that which is actually known to your audience!

DOUBLE FUN

– is it an amazing coincidence – or is it telepathy?

You will need

- Two packs of cards
  - A helper
    - A sharp eye!

The Trick

Having proven your powers of precognition in performing 'Five Alive', your audience will no doubt be keen to see more. Ask to borrow a second pack of cards. Being an expert card magician you will, of course, have your own to hand just in case your friends don't have a spare one. Give one pack to your helper and ask him to shuffle it; you do the same with the other pack. You then exchange packs.

'We are going to attempt an experiment in coincidence and empathy!' you say. 'I want you to look through the cards in your hand and choose one that appeals to you. Make sure you take one from well inside, not from near the bottom, which I might have had a chance to see.

'Take that card from the deck, make sure you memorise it and place it on top of the pack. Now cut the cards somewhere near the middle, placing the cards you have cut on top of your chosen card, thus completely losing it in the deck.'

You now look into your helper's eyes (practise doing this without laughing). 'Hmm… that is very interesting. I will now do exactly the same as you did!'

You look through your deck, removing one card, which you place on top and then cut into the middle.

'Some experts say that sometimes people connect at a subconscious level and are able to exchange information without saying a word. Let's see if we can prove that here and now.'

You exchange decks one more time. You then have your helper go through the cards and remove the duplicate of his chosen card from his deck. You do the same, then you both lay your cards face down on the table.

You ask your helper to turn the cards over – incredibly you have both chosen the same card!

The Secret

One of the most useful weapons in the card magician's armoury is what is called a 'key card'. This is a card that, whilst it isn't usually your helper's chosen card, actually tells you (or gives you a clue as to) which card was selected. Sometimes key cards are specially doctored with marks, cuts or crimps, but in this case we have made our key card on the fly.

Here's what to do. After you have both shuffled and before you hand the deck over to your helper to make his selection, simply glance at the bottom card of the deck. This will be your key card, so make sure you do not forget it. Let's say it was, for example, the Three of Hearts.

Once you have exchanged decks, have your helper select a card from the middle, memorise it, place it on top and cut it to the middle. This places his chosen card next to the Three of Hearts.

Now you make your selection from your deck, but only go through the motions. Do not even try to remember the card you chose, as it will only confuse you. Now when you exchange decks, all you need to do is go through and find the Three of Hearts (your key card). You now know that the

chosen card will be one card below it in the deck. You both lay your cards on the table, show that they are matching and take your applause!

Final Thoughts

There are, in fact, two principles at work in this trick. The first is the key card, and the second is a little known fact about cutting a deck of cards: that when you cut a deck of cards, you don't actually change the order. Thus, with this trick you could have the decks cut several times (this is not really necessary, however, as the effect is strong enough as it stands).

Make sure you practise choosing and cutting cards for yourself so that you become familiar with where the chosen card goes in relation to the key card. Also, make sure that your helper chooses a card from inside the deck – you don't want him or her picking your key card!

What Have We Learned?

That all our words count, and thus we must choose them wisely and use them well!

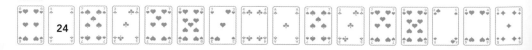

LOOK WHO TURNED UP!
– an amazing display of pasteboard empathy

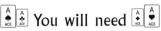 **You will need**
- A pack of cards
- A helper
- To pay attention!

 **The Trick**

Once you have performed a few magic tricks with cards (or anything else for that matter) you will inevitably find your audience asking, 'How did you do that?' If you wish to inject a bit of humour you could simply say, 'Very well, of course!' However, giving a false, or 'cod' explanation (one that sounds plausible but is in fact total nonsense) can open up opportunities for you to perform even more miracles.

After you have performed a trick or two you can begin to explain how some of them work. You can start your explanation by saying something like this.

'As you know, we all have different characters and personalities, yet people tend to choose friends who are in some ways similar to themselves.

'Cards have different personalities too – just think of their suits, numbers, colours and all of the characters they evoke. Perhaps we might tend to choose cards that are somehow like ourselves.'

You begin to sort through the deck and you remove nine cards, which you place in a pile on the table. 'Of course, it might be difficult to do that accurately with a full deck of 52 cards, each one vying for your attention. So we will try this trick using just a few cards.'

You look carefully through the cards you have selected and nod to yourself knowingly. Fan them face down and ask your helper to choose one, look at it and put it straight back on the pile. Next, hand the cards to him and ask him to give them an overhand shuffle so as to make sure no one could know where his card was in the selection.

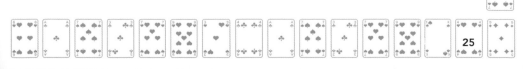

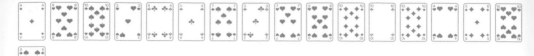

You then lay the cards out face upwards on the table between you and your helper.

You gaze thoughtfully at them and point at one or two, saying, 'Well, you could have chosen the Three of Spades, but that's not really you. The Four of Hearts is closer, but I think your card was the Nine of Hearts!'

Everyone looks astonished, as you are 100 per cent correct!

The Secret

The principle underlying this trick is one that is widely used in card magic. There are specially made trick decks that rely on a similar idea. Likewise, there are even tricks using advertising decks (the ones with products on the back rather than a geometric design), which many magicians know and love. We will touch on these ideas later, but in tricks such as this one what is often overlooked is that the secret is 'in-built' into all decks of cards.

Somewhat confusingly, the concept behind such tricks is known as the 'one-way' principle (a complete misnomer, as you will soon see). Take, for example, the Three of Spades and the Four of Hearts out of your deck and have a good look at them. You will see that the Three of Spades has two pips pointing one way and one pip pointing the other way. Compare this to the Four of Hearts, which has two pips pointing up and two pointing down.

Now swivel the Three of Spades around 180 degrees and then back again a few times, then do the same with the Four of Hearts. You will soon spot that you can tell when the Three of Spades has been turned around because the number of upward pointing pips changes. You can't do that with the Four of Hearts, however, as it looks the same either way up!

So how do we apply this idea? Firstly, we need to choose the right selection of cards. Make them odd-number cards and use any mixture of Hearts, Clubs and Spades, plus one even-number card for good measure. Make sure you also choose a nine (more of which later), and don't choose any Diamonds because the Diamond pips have no distinguishable ups or downs.

Sort through the cards, make your selection and arrange them so that all of the pips on each card point upwards, except the even-number card which can go either way up.

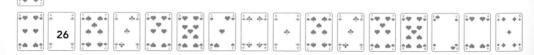

Fan the cards and have one selected. Whilst the card is being looked at, turn the cards in your hand through 180 degrees. Now have the card returned to the packet and hand it out for an overhand shuffle.

Lay the cards out on the table and you will see immediately which card was chosen. As you turned all the other cards around, your helper's card will be pointing the opposite way to the others. If there is no card pointing the other way, then the even-numbered card must have been the one chosen.

Final Thoughts

It goes without saying that this trick needs care and attention when you are performing it. The first thing to get right is the arrangement of the cards: practise doing this a few times so that you can make it seem casual and natural.

Also, make sure you keep an eye on your helper and be sure to follow the chosen card. Sometimes your helper may turn it over for you – just by chance as a result of their natural actions – so be aware!

Make sure your helper knows to give an overhand shuffle. A gesture mimicking the shuffle as you make the request often helps.

One part of the trick you can really have fun with is the moment when you go though the cards on the table, discounting the others. If your helper is a friend, then you can make a few jokes at his expense – all with the best intentions of course.

What Have We Learned?

Sometimes, even when the secret to a trick is staring your audience in the face, they still won't see it.

STRAIGHT TO THE POINT
An intriguing follow-on to your previous miracle.

You will need
- The same set of cards you used in 'Look Who Turned Up!' (*see page 25*)
- A new helper (who is also a secret accomplice)

The Trick

Having just wowed your friends by working out which card they picked, you offer to prove you can go one step further and tell them which card they merely *thought of* while you were in a different room.

You take the same cards you used previously in 'Look Who Turned Up!' (*see page 25*) and lay them out on the table facing upwards. You then give your instructions.

'I am about to leave the room. After I have done so, will you please select one card from those layed out on the table? Do not touch it, please just name it *quietly* so that I cannot possibly hear what you say outside the room.'

You take your leave and, after a few moments, you are called back in. You select another one of your friends to be your helper. Ask this person to point at each of the cards, one at a time, and say that you will try and feel the surge in the psychic energy that should occur when the chosen card is touched.

The helper begins pointing to each card, and on one card your body twitches a little. They carry on, but you ask them to go back to the Five of Spades. Nothing else needs to be said – you have divined the correct card!

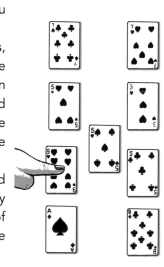

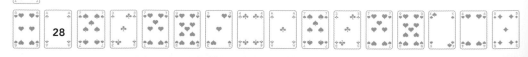

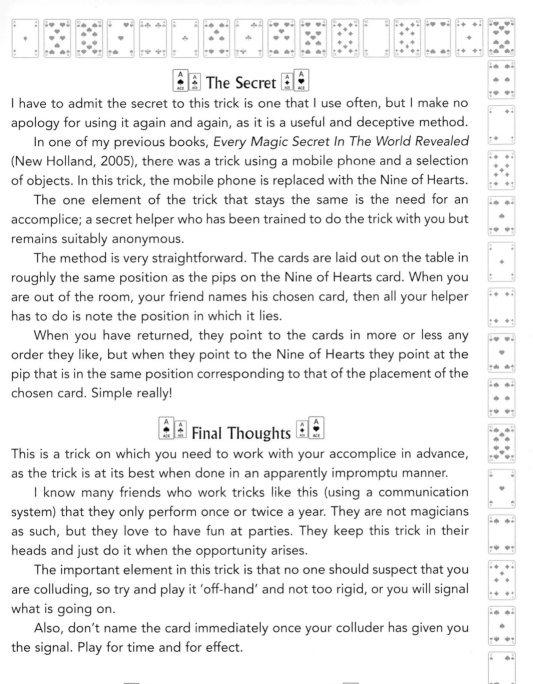

The Secret

I have to admit the secret to this trick is one that I use often, but I make no apology for using it again and again, as it is a useful and deceptive method.

In one of my previous books, *Every Magic Secret In The World Revealed* (New Holland, 2005), there was a trick using a mobile phone and a selection of objects. In this trick, the mobile phone is replaced with the Nine of Hearts.

The one element of the trick that stays the same is the need for an accomplice; a secret helper who has been trained to do the trick with you but remains suitably anonymous.

The method is very straightforward. The cards are laid out on the table in roughly the same position as the pips on the Nine of Hearts card. When you are out of the room, your friend names his chosen card, then all your helper has to do is note the position in which it lies.

When you have returned, they point to the cards in more or less any order they like, but when they point to the Nine of Hearts they point at the pip that is in the same position corresponding to that of the placement of the chosen card. Simple really!

Final Thoughts

This is a trick on which you need to work with your accomplice in advance, as the trick is at its best when done in an apparently impromptu manner.

I know many friends who work tricks like this (using a communication system) that they only perform once or twice a year. They are not magicians as such, but they love to have fun at parties. They keep this trick in their heads and just do it when the opportunity arises.

The important element in this trick is that no one should suspect that you are colluding, so try and play it 'off-hand' and not too rigid, or you will signal what is going on.

Also, don't name the card immediately once your colluder has given you the signal. Play for time and for effect.

What Have We Learned?

Timing and opportunity both play a large part in making magic succeed.

CHAPTER 3
APPLIED FORCE

One of the most useful skills in card magic (in fact, in all magic) is the ability to 'force' an item on your helper. Forcing is where we appear to give them an entirely free choice of something, but in fact we are limiting and controlling that choice in some way.

Over the years, magicians have conceived many thousands of ways to force objects on their audiences, and the vast majority of those forces have been done with cards. This favouritism for card forces has occurred, I think, for two reasons. Firstly, we all know that card tricks are the most popular type of magic we are likely to see. However, we should also recognise that because cards have numerical values, we could employ a card force to force a number, which can then be used to force any object from a numbered list.

But beware! It would be very easy for me to give you a dozen different forces and then tell you that you now have twelve new card tricks for your repertoire, as you could perform each force in turn and reveal a list of your 'predictions'. The weakness in such a performance would be two-fold. Firstly, a force needs to appear as if you are giving a normal, regular choice of card to your helper. If your handling of the selection varies too wildly without good reason, your audience could become a little bit suspicious. Secondly, if one is going to reveal a prediction as the denouement for a trick, then there needs to be sufficient drama and by-play to build up the tension to actually make an effect out of your trick.

So whilst we might know many methods of magic, we can only know as many tricks as we can decently 'perform'. However, the opportunity is there for us to learn many tricks, then choose our best examples to show our audience.

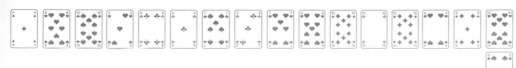

Whilst every procedure for forcing cannot always be re-employed to suit every trick requiring a force, I am convinced that there are far too many forces out there, and that the novice card magician may end up confused by the apparent need to learn a hundred forces when in fact he needs just a few.

Here is a small selection of what are, in my opinion, some of the most useful card forces for any magician to know. They are all different, requiring different skills, and can be used for achieving different effects. For each force I have described a trick (and in one case a brief variation) that illustrates how to use it.

FORCE 13
– a demonstration of your super memory skills

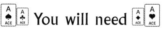 You will need

- A specially arranged deck
- A helper
- An adequate memory!

The Trick

Whilst among a group of friends, you claim that as a magician all your senses and human abilities are trained and refined to a much higher level than those of most people.

You fan out a pack of cards and offer them to your helper. 'Please select a card from the middle of the pack. To be sure no one sees it, even yourself, put it away in your pocket very quickly. I want to show you something with these cards. It's not a card trick in the way you'd normally expect; it is more a demonstration of my photographic memory!'

Your helper does what he is told. You lay the deck on the table and have it cut a couple of times.

'Does anyone here have a second-hand on their watch? You do! That's great! I want you to time something for me.'

You explain that on the word 'Go' you will spread the cards face up on the table. Your helper is to start timing, and after five seconds they must gather up the cards and turn them back over so that they are facing downwards once again.

'Three, two, one, GO!' you say.

You spread the cards on the table, gaze at them and, after five seconds, the cards are gathered up. You immediately start muttering to yourself as if you were counting under your breath. Your eyes are gazing upwards as if you are looking into your mind's eye.

After a few moments you say something quite remarkable. 'I have looked through the picture of the cards in my mind and I can only see one missing, and that is the Six of Hearts. Which card is in your pocket please?'

Your helper pulls the Six of Hearts from inside his coat, proving your memory is spot on!

The Secret

The secret to this trick lies in two parts. Yes, it is a force, but it is not a force of a single card, but rather of a group of cards.

In one of my previous books, *Mind Tricks* (New Holland, 2007), I referred to a mnemonic system for remembering a sequence of cards that uses the word CHaSeD, which of course stands for CLUBS, HEARTS, SPADES and DIAMONDS. We are using that system again here, but in a much simpler form.

From your deck of cards remove the following 13 cards:

Ace of Clubs   Two of Hearts   Three of Spades
Four Of Diamonds   Five of Clubs   Six of Hearts
Seven of Spades   Eight of Diamonds   Nine of Clubs
Ten of Hearts   Jack of Spades   Queen of Diamonds
King of Clubs

You will no doubt have spotted that these cards are arranged in both numerical and CHaSeD order. Spend a little time remembering the sequence. Repeat the list in your head a few times to get the hang of it. Once you can recall the sequence without even thinking, you are almost ready to perform this trick. Arrange these cards in the middle of the deck and you are all set.

Fan the cards towards your helper, requesting that one be chosen from the middle. The secret here is to offer a limited selection of cards to your helper, and to have them fanned out fairly widely. You've guessed it – the selection of cards you offer him are your 13 CHaSeD cards!

Have your helper hide the card he chose in his pocket, and then ask for the cards to be cut (remember, as we mentioned before, cutting does not change the actual order of the cards).

Now when the cards are spread face-up on the table, all you have to look for is your set of cards and quickly note which one is missing. This should be easy to spot from within the twelve CHaSeD cards that remain.

Pretend to count through the cards in your mind and announce the name of the card you didn't spot, which is, of course, the one in your helper's pocket.

🂡🂡 Final Thoughts 🂡🂡

You'll have noticed that this trick isn't really a trick! Having said that, it does require some practice. Remembering the sequence of cards is actually the easy part. Learning how to handle the cards and offering just a portion of the deck is the part you should spend most time on, followed by practice in spotting the missing card.

Occasionally you will encounter a difficult helper who will want to choose a card from elsewhere in the deck. This can, of course, mess up a trick such as this one. So what should you do?

My advice is to let them take the card they want. Let's face it, you can't really stop them. Simply revert to another trick from your repertoire that can be done with any chosen card and carry on as if nothing happened.

What Have We Learned?

By framing any trick as an experiment, any secret setups, moves or odd words tend to be overlooked by your audience.

FORCE 13: THE TELLER'S VARIATION
– a cunning variation of the previous trick!

You will need
- The same set-up as Force 13 (*see page 31*)
  - A helper
  - A telephone
- A friend with a telephone and a good memory!

The Trick

Tell your audience that you have a strange friend who likes to read people's minds from afar. Now have your helper chose a card, which he then hides away in his pocket. Nobody, not even he, knows what the card is.

You spread the cards on the table to show that there is no special arrangement of the cards, and they are indeed all different (sound familiar?).

Now pick up your phone and ask your audience to wait a moment or two whilst you call your friend. Explain that your friend is called 'The Teller', and that he can be a bit grumpy sometimes.

After a few moments the phone is answered. Your audience only hears one side of the conversation, of course. 'Hello, is The Teller there please? Ah, good evening Teller. I have someone here who would like their mind read.'

Your helper takes the phone and listens carefully as The Teller says, 'This is The Teller, and your card is the Seven of Spades.'

For the first time the chosen card is revealed – and the Teller is correct!

The Secret

In the book *Mind Magic* I described one of the first mind-reading tricks I had learned as a young magician. On the face of it, the effect of that trick, called 'Telecommunication', is the same as the one I have just described.

The method involved in 'Telecommunication' and in this trick is one of those secret-code arrangements, similar to the one we've just seen in 'Straight to the Point' (*see page 28*). That trick took a fair bit of setting up, memory work and practice. When done well, it can have a most astounding effect.

If you do not perform very often, however, you might consider it a little too much work for the reward. Thus I offer you this variation, which is a lot simpler to achieve. Once you have learned this variation, the 'Force 13' trick (*see page 31*) should be a breeze to master.

Forcing and learning the card in this variation occurs almost exactly as it does in the 'Force 13' trick, but the rest of the effect uses a secret helper. You will need to recruit such a person, and thereafter you must rehearse the trick using code and a protocol.

Whenever the secret helper's phone rings, that person should listen out for the words, 'Hello, is The Teller there please?' As soon as the secret helper hears these words, they should begin to count, 'Ace, two, three, four…King'.

The moment the value of the chosen card is spoken by the secret helper, you interrupt him and say, 'Ah, good evening Teller…', and hand the phone to your helper. Because of the ChaSeD code (*see pages 32–33*), the secret helper will be able to name the chosen playing card.

Final Thoughts

If there was ever a trick where a good bit of play-acting was useful, this is it! For your part, play it straight, but for your friend playing 'The Teller' there needs to be some good amateur dramatics.

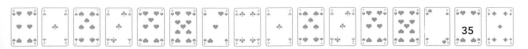

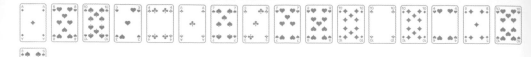

A really good choice of secret helper is another magician because you can play 'The Teller' for each other. Also, such a person will give you somebody reliable to practise with who knows what they are doing.

Two points to bear in mind with this trick are as follows. First of all, make sure you call your secret helper 'The Teller' immediately. In this communications-led age, you don't want to be accused of texting the card over. Secondly, if The Teller doesn't answer the phone, this is not a problem. Pretend that he did, speak to him as if he were there, and announce, 'The Teller believes your card to be the Seven of Spades.'

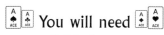 What Have We Learned?

That greater complexity does not always create a better effect!

A LITTLE UNDERHAND
– an amazing three-way prediction of a card

You will need
- 2 helpers
- 2 decks of cards, one blue-backed and one red-backed.
  (One of the decks is a little bit special)
- A sneaky force

The Trick

Choose a couple of helpers from your audience. They must decide between them who will choose a card and who will be the keeper of your predictions.

You now show two decks of cards, one blue-backed and one red-backed. Offer the red one to the 'keeper', telling him it holds your prediction.

Now turn to your other helper whilst shuffling the blue deck and say, 'I want you to choose one card from this randomly mixed deck. And just so

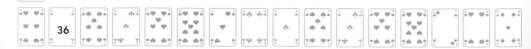

there can be no accusation of me controlling the cards, I am going to hand them to you to do all the work!'

You hand him the cards and ask him to cut off a few from the top, turn them upside down and place them back on top of the deck. 'Now just to make sure the cards are truly randomised, cut the cards again, this time a few more cards than before, reverse them and place them on the top just as before.'

Have him repeat this process a couple of times, giving him the option to stop when he chooses. Now take the cards from him, holding them very gingerly between your thumb and finger and showing the back and front of the pack, which you then lay on the table in front of him.

'Now I want you to go through the cards until you find the first card that is arranged facing downwards with its back towards you. When you find it,

slide it out, but do not look at it just yet. When I said that deck contained my prediction, I wasn't quite telling the truth. You see that deck contains three predictions. Please remove it from the box.

'You will note it is a red-backed deck, but it does contain one blue-backed card, and that is my first prediction – that you will choose a blue-backed card!' Quite rightfully your audience will groan a little here as you spread the cards face down on the table to find one blue-backed card somewhere in the middle.

'But there is more. I was confident that you would choose a blue-backed card, but not just any blue-backed card. Please, each of you, turn over your cards.'

The keeper and the helper each turn their cards over to show that they match perfectly.

'I knew you would both choose the Eight of Spades.'

Your audience will now be a little more appreciative, but you have one last surprise up your sleeve.

'Did you know I was just so confident you would choose the Eight of Spades that I didn't bother having the rest of the cards printed?'

You turn over the red deck and spread it across the table, showing that all the cards are completely blank!

The Secret

This trick requires a force, and yes, you could use any number of different forcing methods to achieve a similar result. In addition, you will need to learn a false shuffle (*see box opposite*). You will also need to buy some special cards.

As you may already know, we magicians have a network of shops and clubs where we can buy and learn new tricks and ideas. (I've given you a few addresses at the back of this book; *see page 95*). In those shops, amongst the wands and top hats, you will find all manner of specially printed playing cards. So make a journey (in real life or online) to one of these shops and buy yourself a blank-faced deck. This is simply a deck with a printed back but nothing on the front.

Choose a deck with a back colour or design that contrasts with your 'normal' cards, and slip in one normal card as your prediction. Keep that card with you, ready to hand out when you perform.

THE FALSE SHUFFLE

The basic idea behind a false shuffle is that you apparently shuffle the cards into a random order, but in reality you secretly keep them in order. Many variations exist, but here is a simple false shuffle that will suit the various tricks in this book.

Hold the deck in your right hand with the faces of the cards upwards. With your left thumb, draw off three cards and let them fall into the left hand. Then, whilst continuing the same motion, drop the remainder of the deck onto the three cards in your left hand. Take the deck back into the right hand and repeat the process, this time counting off four cards and, again, dropping the deck onto them.

Now pause for a second and casually turn the whole deck over while passing it from the left hand to the right. The deck will now have its back facing towards you. Count off three cards just as before, dropping the deck onto them. Then repeat with four cards just as you did previously. What you have done is to move seven cards from the front to the back of the deck and then immediately return them to their original places.

You may think that what you have done will be obvious to your audience, but if you follow two golden rules it will not be. First, always look at your audience while you are shuffling. Never look at the cards. Practise until you can do this confidently. Second, never say 'I am shuffling the cards', as this will call attention to them. Just shuffle and people will simply remember that you shuffled the deck!

The force we use here is known as the 'Cut Deeper' force. The reason for this somewhat strange name will become obvious as I explain how it works: Take your normal deck of cards in your hand right now. Look at the top card and remember it. Cut off a few cards and turn them over on top of the deck. Repeat this action three more times, each time cutting off more cards – and thereby 'cutting deeper'.

Now run through the face up cards until you arrive at the first face down card. Does that card ring a bell? It will be the card from the top of the deck.

Now reset the cards and repeat the process, only this time cut and turn the cards five times. You will see that the top card is now the last card before

the first face down card. Of course, if you turn the whole deck upside down, the top card is once more the first face down card.

Simply put, if the cards are turned an even number of times, the top card will end up as the first face down card. If they are turned an odd number of times, the top card will end up immediately before the first face down card.

Thus, in order to force your card (the duplicate of the card you placed in the blank deck), first place it at the top of the deck. Give the cards a casual false shuffle *(see box on page 39)* and hand them to your helper.

Have the cards cut and turned, making sure you ask for them to be cut deeper each time. Within reason, you can allow your helper to choose when to stop turning. (Of course, you don't want him to go too far as this will be boring, and you will run out of cards.) Just make sure that you note whether the cards were turned an odd or even number of times.

Take the cards back between your thumb and forefinger, apparently to display them fairly. In fact, you are taking them so that you can lay them down on the table the correct way around so as to leave the force card as the first face down card. Your force is now complete. All you need do now is reveal your predictions with a bit of showmanship.

Final Thoughts

I should explain why the Cut Deeper force is a good choice for this trick. There are thousands of forces, but they follow a limited number of plots.

For a direct prediction such as this one, a force in which the magician fans the cards and has one selected is not appropriate, as it seems to signal that a force is going on. In contrast, the force used in this trick is actually done by your helper, and thus it seems natural and fair.

Furthermore, in this force there is a correlation between the states of the chosen card and the prediction. They both appear to be in some way displaced in the deck, and thus there is some subtle connection that makes the trick a little more believable.

If you can't find a supplier of trick cards, don't worry – simply use a normal red-backed deck and reverse your prediction card in it. I'm sure you can work out some suitable patter for yourself.

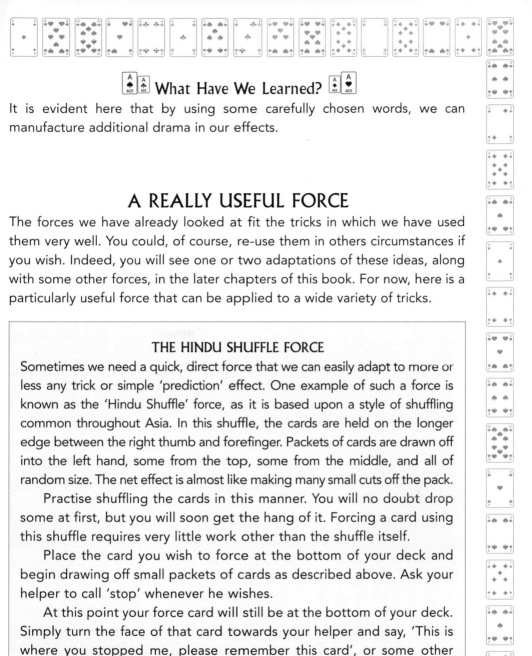

What Have We Learned?

It is evident here that by using some carefully chosen words, we can manufacture additional drama in our effects.

A REALLY USEFUL FORCE

The forces we have already looked at fit the tricks in which we have used them very well. You could, of course, re-use them in others circumstances if you wish. Indeed, you will see one or two adaptations of these ideas, along with some other forces, in the later chapters of this book. For now, here is a particularly useful force that can be applied to a wide variety of tricks.

THE HINDU SHUFFLE FORCE

Sometimes we need a quick, direct force that we can easily adapt to more or less any trick or simple 'prediction' effect. One example of such a force is known as the 'Hindu Shuffle' force, as it is based upon a style of shuffling common throughout Asia. In this shuffle, the cards are held on the longer edge between the right thumb and forefinger. Packets of cards are drawn off into the left hand, some from the top, some from the middle, and all of random size. The net effect is almost like making many small cuts off the pack.

Practise shuffling the cards in this manner. You will no doubt drop some at first, but you will soon get the hang of it. Forcing a card using this shuffle requires very little work other than the shuffle itself.

Place the card you wish to force at the bottom of your deck and begin drawing off small packets of cards as described above. Ask your helper to call 'stop' whenever he wishes.

At this point your force card will still be at the bottom of your deck. Simply turn the face of that card towards your helper and say, 'This is where you stopped me, please remember this card', or some other similar words that are suitable for your presentation.

Place the cards in your right hand on top of those in your left and the apparently free choice of card is now lost in the pack!

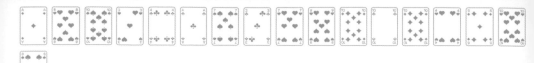

A little later on in the book we will be showing you how to get your force cards to the bottom or top of the pack with consummate ease (*see pages 59–61*).

A REAL TOUR DE FORCE

So we now know a couple of great ways to force a card or cards on our helpers.

It is worth knowing a variety of forces so that you can make suitable choices about which ones to use for your own tricks. I could fill a whole book with nothing but card forces, but I won't do so here! You will, however, find one or two more methods in this book as we go along.

The most important thing to learn when forcing is that you can't get away with just forcing a card and then immediately revealing a prediction. You will look like a bad or cocky magician, and I am sure you don't want to be known as either. You need to add timing, drama and perhaps some comedy into your act in order to sell a force.

If you're really keen to get a handle on a wide variety of forces, I would direct your attention to the further reading section of this book (*see page 95*), where you will find a list of great books that detail other methods of forcing.

Now let's see how a few secrets can add up to real magic…

CHAPTER 4
IT ALL ADDS UP TO MAGIC

At some point in your card-magic career you will find yourself experiencing rejection. It is a kind of rite of passage we all have to go through. It may be tough, but we become better performers for having heard the words, 'Oh no, not a card trick. Card tricks are boring!' and getting over it with a reasonably intact ego. Usually we hear these words just as we have enthusiastically taken our trusty deck from our pocket.

But why do we hear this phrase so often? Well in my opinion it is down to people's experience of seeing a great trick performed remarkably badly. One common example is the trick your grandfather or uncle probably showed you: where the cards are laid out into rows and, after counting them back and forth for what seems like hours, he finally reveals your choice of card. Quite often, all that hard work will have been for nothing because he will reveal the wrong card anyway!

This trick is known by many names, but most often as the Twenty-One Card Trick. It relies upon a mathematical principle to make it work. Your uncle has probably made two mistakes in showing you this trick. His first error was in assuming that he needs to do nothing to add to the trick because the numbers will do all the work. More importantly, he only performs it once a year, and thus he is unsure or unfamiliar with its workings and runs a high risk of messing up.

Because of such past experiences you could be forgiven for wishing to avoid tricks with a mathematical element.

This chapter shows us that we don't need a lot of moves to create strong magic. But it also warns us that simply going through the mechanics of a trick only gives the illusion of an amateur playing at being a magician. In this chapter I am going to present to you some classic mathematical tricks that I hope give you a sense of place and

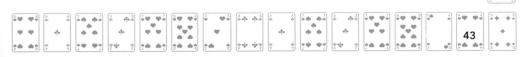

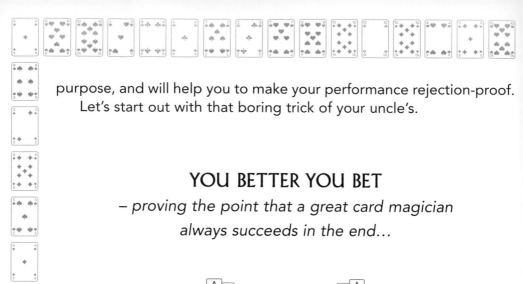

purpose, and will help you to make your performance rejection-proof. Let's start out with that boring trick of your uncle's.

YOU BETTER YOU BET
– proving the point that a great card magician
always succeeds in the end...

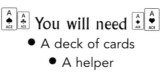 You will need
- A deck of cards
- A helper

The Trick

Choose a helper and offer him a chance to win some money from you. Lay your wager (a coin) on the table, then say, 'I am going to try and guess where your chosen card will be. Would you please deal out three columns of seven cards each, facing up on the table.'

Your helper does as he is asked. You then ask him to mentally select one of the twenty-one cards he can now see. You then think for a minute and point to one of the columns, announcing, 'I bet your card is in this line!' The smile soon fades from your face, however, as he shakes his head, indicating you are wrong.

'Oh dear. You win the bet. Which line was it in please?' He points to the column with his card. You give him the coin you owe him, then gather all three lines up in your hand and ask him to lay them out again. 'You won that time,' you say, 'but let's play double or quits.'

You ponder for a moment and point to a different line. 'Your card is in this line!' Again, he shakes his head. You have lost two bets in a row.

Once again the cards are gathered up and laid on the table. Rather less than amazingly, you get it right on your third attempt.

'OK,' you say. 'I didn't do very well but I think I can up the ante a little here.'

The cards are gathered up and laid out again, one last time, and you now turn your back for a moment.

'I want you to place the coin you won from our original bet on your chosen card. Have you done that? Good. Your chosen card was the Six of Spades.'

You turn around and find a shiny gold coin sitting atop the Six of Spades.

♠ ♦ The Secret ♦ ♥

There really isn't much of a secret to this one, as it works mathematically. However, you must be mindful of the need to gather and lay the cards out correctly each time. You also need to be aware that the patter will vary each time you perform this trick, so you need to be alert.

Let's go through the mechanics first. All the handling, dealing and gathering of the cards should be done face up. Now hold the deck face upwards in your hand and deal three cards in a row, which we will call A, B and C.

Start dealing a second row by placing another card on top of card A, then one more on B and the next on C. Keep going until you have three columns, each containing seven cards. Now try the trick yourself by thinking of one of the cards in the columns. Don't move the card – just note which column it is in. Now gather up the three columns, making sure that the column with your card in it is placed between the other two columns.

Deal the cards into the three columns once again. You will see that they are now in a different order and layout, and that your chosen card may or may not be in a different column. Either, way gather up the cards, again making sure that the column with your card in it goes between the other two. Deal out the cards again just as before.

Now gather up the cards for the last time, following the same rules as before and, finally, deal out the cards in exactly the same manner. Provided you have followed the outlined procedure, your card will be the middle card in the middle column.

Once you are certain of the mechanics of this trick, you need to practise it, so spend a little time having a friend or your partner go through it with you.

The rest of the trick is just presentation. Of course, you have no way of knowing at the outset which column the card is in. Sometimes you will be right and sometimes you will be wrong. You thus need to be prepared to adjust your patter accordingly.

If you get it right, you can say, 'That's good, I won.' Then gather up the cards, knowing which column to place in the middle. You can then say, 'I think I should give you another chance.' This allows you to carry on and repeat the trick in order to get to the conclusion.

If you miss, however, then you say, 'Oh dear, you win. Which column was it in this time?' Again, you know how to gather the cards up. You can then say, 'Perhaps you will give me another chance to win my bet back?'

Either way, play it cool and make everything seem as if it just flows.

I want to give you one warning with this trick. Sometimes when you are practising it you may notice that the chosen card gets into the middle position on the second or third layout of the cards. This can happen depending upon where it started out, but remember that you only notice it because it is your chosen card. In an actual performance you must go through the whole procedure in order to be certain that you know which card was selected.

Final Thoughts

I have previously written up a similar trick up in another one of my books (*How to be a Mind Magician*, Tobar, 2005) and, in that case, it was presented

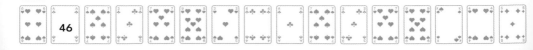

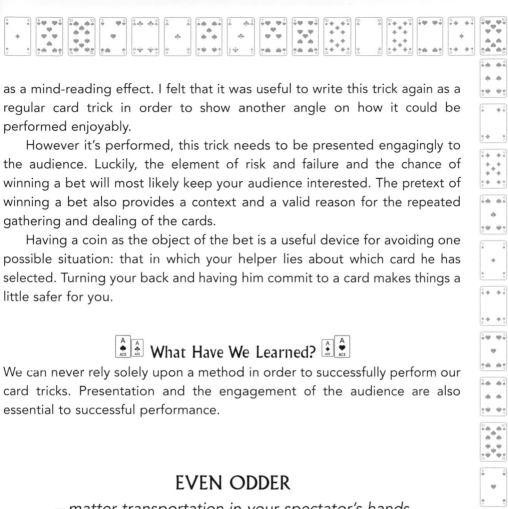

as a mind-reading effect. I felt that it was useful to write this trick again as a regular card trick in order to show another angle on how it could be performed enjoyably.

However it's performed, this trick needs to be presented engagingly to the audience. Luckily, the element of risk and failure and the chance of winning a bet will most likely keep your audience interested. The pretext of winning a bet also provides a context and a valid reason for the repeated gathering and dealing of the cards.

Having a coin as the object of the bet is a useful device for avoiding one possible situation: that in which your helper lies about which card he has selected. Turning your back and having him commit to a card makes things a little safer for you.

What Have We Learned?

We can never rely solely upon a method in order to successfully perform our card tricks. Presentation and the engagement of the audience are also essential to successful performance.

EVEN ODDER

– matter transportation in your spectator's hands

You will need
- A deck of cards
  - A helper
- To go with the flow

The Trick

You open your performance with an unusual line. 'You will hear many magicians open their performance by saying they are going to show you

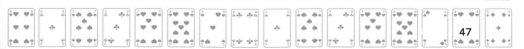

something atypical or odd. Well, today I am going to do the complete opposite. I'm going to show you something even!'

You ask your helper to sit opposite you at the table and to lay his hands just as if he was playing the piano. 'Keep your hands still, please, as I am going to give you some thing to hold on to.'

You wedge two cards between the third and little finger on the helper's left hand. 'Here is a pair of cards, so this is EVEN…' You continue placing three more pairs of cards each between the remaining three gaps in his left hand.

'This is EVEN, this is EVEN and this is EVEN, too.'

You then turn to your helper's right hand and do the same, starting again with the gap between the third and little fingers.

'This is EVEN, this is EVEN, this is EVEN, but…' You now place a single card between the forefinger and thumb of your helper's right hand.

'This one is ODD!'

You then remove one pair from the left hand and lay them out on the table in front of the helper; lay one card on his left and the other on his right. Again, you say, 'This is EVEN.' And you continue removing all the pairs of cards, one at a time, laying them down left and right, saying, 'This is EVEN' until you have two piles of cards. Leave the odd card in your helper's hand.

'Please lay the ODD card on either pile. You decide which.'

He lays it on the left-hand pile. 'Are you sure you know where you put that last card?' you ask. You helper seems bemused, of course, as he just placed the card on the left-hand pile a second ago. You count out the cards from the left-hand pile, two at a time. 'Here is a pair, so this is EVEN, this is EVEN, this is EVEN and this is EVEN. It seems our odd card has vanished!'

You then count out the right-hand pile. 'This is EVEN, this is EVEN, this is EVEN, but we have just one card left – now isn't that ODD!'

♠♣ The Secret ♠♥

This trick really does work itself. Even so, it is your patter that sells the trick. Try it for yourself now – you don't need a helper.

Lie out seven pairs of cards and put one odd card in front of you. Take each pair in turn, placing one card on the left and the other on the right.

48

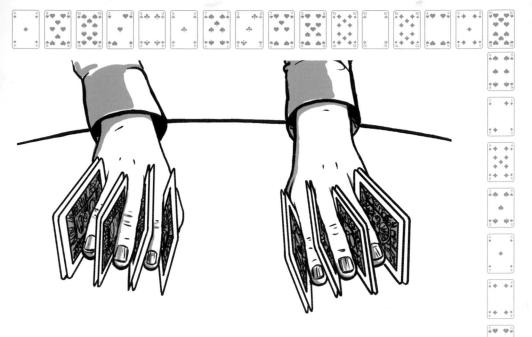

Finally, place the remaining odd card on either pile. Now deal out the piles in pairs again. The pile on which you just placed the odd card now consists of pairs, and the other (which you just made up with pairs) has an odd card.

Most people, including knowledgeable magicians, often confuse themselves with this kind of trick. The result seems to defy the logic. This is, of course, because we all look at things superficially. Think again about the middle phase of the trick, when you separate the cards into the left and right pairs. What are you actually doing? You are, of course, making two piles of seven cards. They are not even pairs at all, but placing the odd card on one pile will make that pile even.

You see – you really are a great magician. You can even fool yourself!

Final Thoughts

It goes without saying that you need to familiarise yourself with the mechanics of this trick to get the order of events clear in your mind.

The real selling point here is your choice of words. Note the overt repetition of the word 'EVEN'. This word constantly reinforces the concept of the cards being in pairs at every stage. So don't change your words halfway through – use this same phrase throughout the trick.

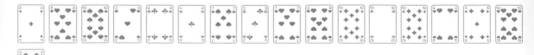

It might help to further cement the pair concept if, once you have placed the cards in your helper's hands, you say, 'Let's go over that again. This is EVEN…' pointing to each set of cards one more time.

Of course this trick doesn't need to be done with cards. You could use coins, matches, cocktail sticks or even business cards.

What Have We Learned?

We have learned here that we should not dismiss too readily what appears to be an obvious method.

A RIGHT PAIR
– a pair of freely chosen cards is divined in an instant

You will need
- A deck of cards (that you have prepared)
- A helper with average mathematical ability
- A pen and paper
- A little mental agility

The Trick

Fan out a pack of cards. Ask your helper to select two cards and place them down on the table without looking at them just yet.

'If I wanted to know what these cards are I could just look at them, but that would not be very magical. You could shuffle them into the deck and I could find them by sleight of hand, but you have seen that before. What I want to do is read your mind, and to do that, I need to get your mind working for me.'

You ask your helper to look at the first card and make a note of its value. 'I want you to do some calculations for me – doing this will help to get your

brain processes working well. You can use this pen and paper if you like, but if you can do the calculations in your head, all the better.'

Ask your helper to double the value of the card (i.e. if it were a 2, double it to make it 4), then to add 5. Now take that answer and multiply it by 5. Then ask him to look at the second card and simply add the value of that card to the total. 'Now please tell me the final sum of your calculations,' you say. He answers, '70.'

'That is interesting because I get the feeling your first card was a 4, but I am not sure if you chose the Spade or the Club – it was the Spade, wasn't it?'

He nods and you continue your revelations. 'The second card is a little tougher. It couldn't be the Five of Hearts, could it? NO…it was the Five of Diamonds.' You are, of course, spot on. So how do you do it?

The Secret

I first played with this trick probably 30 years ago, but soon dismissed it as the version I learned was somewhat bland. Cards were chosen and the calculations done and cards named. The suit of the cards was never given, just the value (i.e. 'You chose a 4 and a 5.').

But here is a lesson for you in creating your own new tricks. You may recall that we used a set-up bank of cards earlier on in this book. Well, it suddenly occurred to me that we could use the same idea here to strengthen the effect, and also to provide a method of learning how to read your audience.

Let's look at the basics of the trick first. In our example, your helper chose a 4 and then a 5. Do the math with me now. He chose a 4; so double it, making 8. Add 5 to make 13 and multiply this by 5 to give us 65. Finally, add the value of the second card, which was 5, to make a total of 70. Now there is one final bit of the calculation that we keep to ourselves: we must subtract 25 from the answer we are given. In this case, we are left with 45. So, quite simply, this number tells us that our first card was a 4 and the second, a 5.

Easy really!

But how do we know the suits, and how do we deal with the court cards? Again, the answer is simple. We need to prepare the deck by creating a

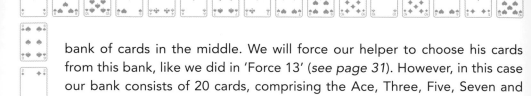

bank of cards in the middle. We will force our helper to choose his cards from this bank, like we did in 'Force 13' (*see page 31*). However, in this case our bank consists of 20 cards, comprising the Ace, Three, Five, Seven and Nine of Hearts and Diamonds and the Two, Four, Six, Eight and Ten of Clubs and Spades.

Shuffle these cards together and position them in the middle of the deck, ready for your selections to be made. Have your helper go through the calculations and give you his answer. By subtracting 25, you will know the values of the cards but not exactly which suit they belong to. However, you do know that the card is an even value if it is a Spade or a Club, and it is odd if it is a Heart or a Diamond.

Now a little verbal byplay comes into force. Note the words used in the example: 'I know it's a 4 but I am not sure if it is a Spade or a Club.' Your audience will be impressed that you are so close anyway, and if you pace your words correctly (slow, clear and even), your helper will often signal which is right as he will furrow his forehead a little and then raise it when you name the correct suit.

Also, think about the line, 'It couldn't be the Five of Hearts, could it?' Your audience cannot be sure whether that was an actual question or a rhetorical question, so either way you end up correct.

Another good line to use is, 'Most people choose the Five of Hearts...' and wait for a reaction. If you get a look of recognition, you are home and dry. If you don't get that look, continue with, 'But you are not like most people – you chose the Five of Diamonds.'

Have fun and learn to play with your words for even better card magic!

🂡🃑 Final Thoughts 🂡🃑

There are many texts on magic which deal with what we call *equivoque* – that is, playing with two or more possible outcomes and making it seem as if we were always headed for the correct one. Look some up and experiment with how this concept can be applied to other tricks you do. There are some useful tips on this in my previous book, *Mind Magic* (New Holland, 2003).

I suggest that you learn to do the maths for this trick in your head. It

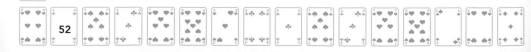

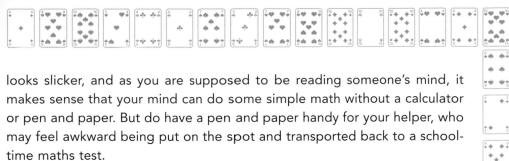

looks slicker, and as you are supposed to be reading someone's mind, it makes sense that your mind can do some simple math without a calculator or pen and paper. But do have a pen and paper handy for your helper, who may feel awkward being put on the spot and transported back to a school-time maths test.

One thing you might need to make clear is that an Ace has a value of 1. In some card games, such as Blackjack, it has a value of 10, so make sure that everyone knows what you mean.

What Have We Learned?

That sometimes our audience and helpers give us more help than they consciously realise!

A FORTUNATE PREDICTION

– *a bit of pseudo fortune-telling using playing cards*

You will need

- A pack of cards
- A notepad
- A pen or pencil
- A specially prepared short card
- A helper (who might need a calculator)
- A written prediction

The Trick

Having shown a few tricks, you now begin to explain some of the mystical properties of cards and how they can be used to read people's fortunes. You hand a small slip of paper to your helper and ask him to keep it safe for a

while. Then you give him a pack of cards to shuffle and, just for good measure, you shuffle them too.

Ask your helper to write down his birth year on a notepad, and then to jumble up the digits in that number to make a new random number, which he should also write down.

For example, if he was born in 1981, he should write that number as well as a scrambled version of that year – say 1198.

Now ask your helper to subtract the smaller number from the larger one – taking our example, that would mean subtracting 1198 from 1981, which leaves 783.

'We must now find our significant number using the science of Numerology. We can do this by continually adding the digits in our sum together time after time, until we are left with just one single digit.'

Your helper should then add up the digits.

Using our example, he would add 7, 8 and 3 together to make 18, and then add 1 and 8 to make his final answer of 9.

'Please count through the deck and remove the ninth card. Ahh…your special card is the Ace of Diamonds! This shows that you like to be "numero uno", and that you are bright, sharp and to the point. You are also well defined, but you are sometimes a little cautious in your outlook. Please open the slip of paper I gave your earlier.'

Your helper's jaw will drop as he sees written there 'The Ace of Diamonds, number one, sharp and to the point but sometimes cautious.'

The Secret

I have included this trick at this point in the book as it not only uses a mathematical idea – it also prepares us to move into using some sleight of hand. Don't panic – this is easy to do!

Let's deal with the mathematical part first.

To use myself as an example, I was born in 1961. Now I must scramble the digits to make another number – let's say 1196. Subtracting the smaller number from the larger one, I get 1961 - 1196 = 765. Now add 7 + 6 + 5 = 18, then add 1 + 8 = 9. You see, we have a force for the number 9!

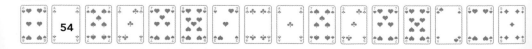

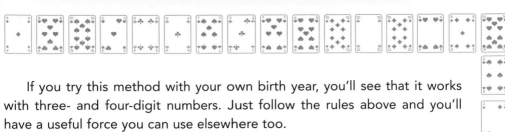

If you try this method with your own birth year, you'll see that it works with three- and four-digit numbers. Just follow the rules above and you'll have a useful force you can use elsewhere too.

But the big question is, of course, how do we know which card is at position nine?

Well, we use a variation of the false shuffle we already learned (*see page 39*), and a specially prepared force card known as a 'short card' (*see page 15*). You can make your card into a short card by trimming a millimetre off one end of the card, which is easy to do using a small guillotine or a ruler and craft knife.

You can use any card you like; in our example, the Ace of Diamonds gave me something interesting to talk about.

Now take your short card and shuffle it into the middle of the pack. Slowly riffle your thumb along the short edge of the deck. You will feel a sudden click, and the deck will stop right at your short card.

Practise this a few times and then move to the next stage, which is cutting the deck at the point where it stops. Your short card will now be on top of the deck.

Now give the cards a false shuffle, only in this case just run eight cards from the bottom of the deck onto the top. Your short card is now in the ninth position!

Once you have mastered all of the above, you are almost ready to perform, but you have one other thing to practise: your patter.

Try and make it relevant to the card you have selected as your force card, and always make your false readings polite and positive.

Final Thoughts

Although there was a fair amount of setting up needed to perform this trick, it can be done more or less impromptu with a little thought. All you have to do is to take on board some of the lessons that you learned from the earlier tricks in this book.

For example, if we can glimpse the bottom card and shuffle it to the ninth position in a borrowed pack, we can create almost exactly the same effect. Yes, we forgo the element of the helper shuffling, but the impact of using a borrowed pack will more than compensate for any potential loss of impact.

Now that we have our short card, why not think about using it as a key card to follow another selection. With this powerful tool now we can cut straight to a chosen card – more of which later.

What Have We Learned?

When we talk about our audience during a trick we must choose our words carefully. It always pays to make positive comparisons. We are, after all, entertainers and we are not here to make enemies.

CHAPTER 5
'SLEIGHTLY TRICKIER'

About half of the tricks in my professional repertoire involve some form of sleight of hand (*see page 14*); the other half relies upon a cocktail of other forms of trickery. Somewhat oddly, no matter which type of trick I am performing I am often credited as having 'very fast hands', whether or not sleight of hand was used.

Audiences typically have a very limited understanding of the mechanics of magic, but they do know about this thing called the 'sleight of hand'; often when they are baffled by a trick they can only assume that some sleight of hand was involved in the trickery.

One could conclude from this fact that you need not learn any sleights to be a good magician. To be honest, you might get away with it, but you may at some time find yourself constrained by not having the confidence to perform a secret move. I have found that the ability to pull off a sleight of hand at the spur of the moment has been a lifesaver when things haven't gone according to plan during a performance.

Dictionaries typically define sleight of hand as 'clever' or 'fast' moves used in conjuring or juggling. This is not an entirely accurate definition, however, as not all sleights are clever, many are very simple and certainly not all are fast!

Of course, the definition we see in dictionaries is a layman's view, and we should outwardly accept it, as it implies we are clever and quick with our hands. However, as magicians, within our secret conclave we need to realise that any secret move we do with cards or other props counts as sleight of hand. This is so because we need to ensure that we understand the move thoroughly, and we need to practise it to make sure that we can execute it accurately and, of course, secretly.

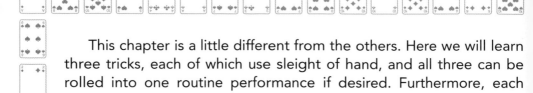

This chapter is a little different from the others. Here we will learn three tricks, each of which use sleight of hand, and all three can be rolled into one routine performance if desired. Furthermore, each trick uses one or two sleights that can be reused in many of the other tricks you will learn in this book and elsewhere.

But don't constrain yourself by simply performing these tricks as you see them here. Move the ingredients for your 'cocktail' around and see how they can spice up some of your other tricks!

CONTROL FREAK
– a little 'mind control' goes a long way

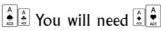 You will need

- A pack of cards
- A helper
- A pen or pencil
- A special card control
- A little bit of verbal by-play

The Trick

Spread a deck of cards towards your helper, asking them to select a card, which they should look at and memorise. Now ask your helper to sign the front of the card. Have your helper place the card randomly into the middle of the pack, which is shuffled and cut a couple of times by you. Hand the deck back to your helper.

'As card expert I need to be in control of both the cards and my helpers. Let me give you a demonstration. Please deal two piles of cards onto the table. Place as many cards in each pile as you wish, but ensure that each pile contains a different number of cards.'

You helper does as requested, then places the rest of the deck aside.

'Now place a forefinger on each of the piles and tell me...

'Was the card you signed a free choice of card?

'Was that free card signed by you, so that there is no other card like it in the world?

'Did you place the card where you wished to in the deck, and were the cards further mixed and shuffled?

'Did you have a free choice as to the numbers of cards in these piles?'

Your helper's head has nodded throughout your questions!

'You now have two piles of cards trapped by your fingers. Lift one hand and free one pile, leaving the other one trapped.'

Your helper frees one pile. You slowly turn over the pile he has freed, and there is his chosen card at the bottom for all to see.

'I have made you free your chosen card! You see, I was in control all along!'

The Secret

This trick is straightforward and simple, but it does require a little sleight of hand plus some time misdirection.

A card is chosen and signed, then it is lost in the deck. You 'control' (*see below*) the chosen card to the top position in the deck, after which the cards are dealt into two piles. The chosen card now lies at the bottom of one of the two piles. You then use a verbal control to imply that your helper makes a free selection of that pile.

THE CARD CONTROL

I have learned dozens of controls over the years, but the one I use if I need to control a card is known as the 'Double Undercut'.

First, we need to practise dribbling the cards from one hand to the other. Hold the deck of cards face down in your left hand. Now pick up the deck in your right hand with the thumb at one end, the second finger at the other and the forefinger in the middle. Bend the ends of the deck slightly upwards and allow the cards to dribble, a few at a time, into your left hand. Practise this action until you can do it smoothly.

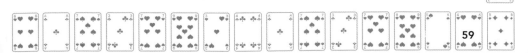

Now here's what you do to make the control happen: have a card selected and, whilst holding the deck in your left hand, pick the cards up, ready to dribble, and ask your helper to call 'stop' whenever he likes.

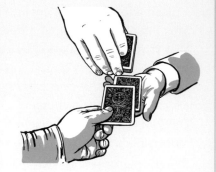

When your helper has called stop, gently squeeze the cards in your left hand, making them into a neat packet. Have your helper place the card on top of this packet.

Now dribble the remainder of the deck onto the card, but in a haphazard manner. This will leave an untidy packet of cards on top of the deck, which is out-jogged from the neat packet with the card on top.

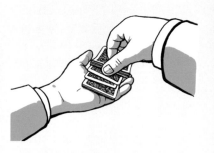

Pick up the whole deck again in the right hand, just as before, and you will see that, with a little practice, you will create a break between the two packets almost automatically! Now, with the left hand, remove about half of the lower packet and place it on the top of the deck. Repeat this with the second half of

the packet, and, of course, the chosen card is now on top of the deck. Now throw in a false shuffle (*see page 39*) for good measure. To your audience, it will seem as if the card was placed at a random point in the deck, which was cut and shuffled.

A final tip here is to keep looking your helper in the eye. Do not focus on the cards – you will only draw attention to your secret moves. This trick takes some practice, but it is completely disarming and deceptive.

THE VERBAL CONTROL

To recap, we now have two piles of cards, one of which contains the chosen card at the bottom. Our helper has a finger placed on the top of each pile.

The first thing you need to do is to identify which pile contains the chosen card. Because it was at the top of the deck, it will, of course, be the first card dealt out by your helper, so simply watch and observe.

Now you have to multitask. Begin saying, 'You now have two piles of cards trapped by your fingers. Lift one hand and free one pile, leaving the other trapped...' and note which pile he releases. If he releases the pile with the card in it, then say, as above, 'I have made you free your chosen card.' If he releases the other pile, say, 'I have made you trap your chosen card.'

The important thing here is to make whatever you say seem like one sentence – don't pause or stutter, and certainly don't make it seem as though you are waiting to see which pile your helper releases. In other words, make your patter flow and you will sell this effect.

Final Thoughts

There are thousands of ways of producing or displaying a selected card. Usually there is a prerequisite need to control that card to a known position in order to effect the revelation. Thus, the card control you have learned is a very useful tool, and will work in place of other card controls that you might see associated with tricks in other books.

You may find yourself asking why not use a force or mathematical method to create the same effect? The answer is that you clearly could do so, but understanding all the basic methods and principles of card magic will help you build better and more effective routines as you progress.

Another valid question is, why sign the card? It is not absolutely necessary to do so, but it adds a degree of mystery because it might be plausible (in our audience's mind) for you to create this effect using duplicate cards. Signing can be an important effect in more complex routines.

While we are on the subject, you may be wondering why we asked so many questions about the helper's free choice. The answer is simple – time misdirection. An immediate revelation of the card would leave the memories

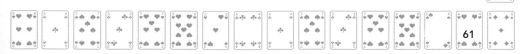

of what had happened fresh in the audience's mind, making it easier to backtrack and to possibly work out the method. Speaking of which, while this is a great little trick, I suggest you follow on with something else immediately!

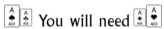 What Have We Learned?

We should become familiar with all the tools available to us so that we can always select the correct one for the job at hand.

LIFT UP!
– you can't keep a good card down!

You will need
- A pack of cards
- Three special moves
- A bit of practice

The Trick

Having just performed the previous trick, 'Control Freak', you gather up the cards and shuffle them, losing the chosen card in the deck once again.

'I hope you liked that last demonstration, but you know that your card is well trained, and I can make it do almost anything!' You spread the cards and show that the previously selected card is neither at the top nor bottom of the deck, but simply by riffling the cards it magically appears on the face of the deck.

Now you take the card and place it fairly and squarely in the middle of the deck, yet with another flick it is at the top of the deck! Once again the card is placed in the middle of the deck and again it rises straight to the top.

Finally, the card is inserted into the deck at your helper's chosen location, and the deck is given to him to hold. You ask him to check and yes, his card has risen to the top in his own hands!

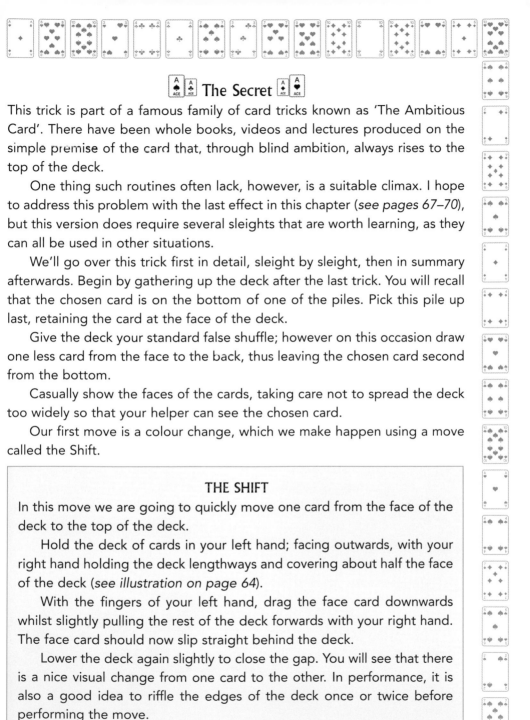

🂡🂡 The Secret 🂡🂡

This trick is part of a famous family of card tricks known as 'The Ambitious Card'. There have been whole books, videos and lectures produced on the simple premise of the card that, through blind ambition, always rises to the top of the deck.

One thing such routines often lack, however, is a suitable climax. I hope to address this problem with the last effect in this chapter (*see pages 67–70*), but this version does require several sleights that are worth learning, as they can all be used in other situations.

We'll go over this trick first in detail, sleight by sleight, then in summary afterwards. Begin by gathering up the deck after the last trick. You will recall that the chosen card is on the bottom of one of the piles. Pick this pile up last, retaining the card at the face of the deck.

Give the deck your standard false shuffle; however on this occasion draw one less card from the face to the back, thus leaving the chosen card second from the bottom.

Casually show the faces of the cards, taking care not to spread the deck too widely so that your helper can see the chosen card.

Our first move is a colour change, which we make happen using a move called the Shift.

THE SHIFT

In this move we are going to quickly move one card from the face of the deck to the top of the deck.

Hold the deck of cards in your left hand; facing outwards, with your right hand holding the deck lengthways and covering about half the face of the deck (*see illustration on page 64*).

With the fingers of your left hand, drag the face card downwards whilst slightly pulling the rest of the deck forwards with your right hand. The face card should now slip straight behind the deck.

Lower the deck again slightly to close the gap. You will see that there is a nice visual change from one card to the other. In performance, it is also a good idea to riffle the edges of the deck once or twice before performing the move.

You have now made the chosen card appear magically at the face of the deck, and you will now apparently take the chosen card and place it face down on top of the deck. In fact, however, you will take two cards using a move called the Double-Lift.

THE DOUBLE-LIFT

There are many methods for a Double-Lift, but I only use the one I learned 30 years ago. Essentially, a Double-Lift involves lifting two cards away so that they appear to be one single card.

The first stage is to get a break, separating the two cards we wish to display as one from the rest of the deck. Hold the deck in the left hand with the right hand across it, just like in the Shift (*see above*). Riffle up the corner of the deck with the right thumb, but do this slowly, so you can feel the cards. When you get to the last two cards, bend your left little finger just slightly inwards so that it can slip between the two cards and the deck. Now your right hand can grasp the top and bottom edges of the two cards, lifting them away as one.

Practice this move. It will take time to get right, but keep working at it until it looks natural. When you feel a bit more adventurous, try turning the card around and from back to front. Remember, you can Double-Lift from the face or top of the deck!

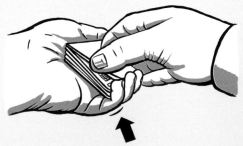

Once you feel confident with using this move, take your

'double card' and place it face down on the top of the deck, so that the chosen card is second from the top (although your audience will think it is the top card). Now remove the top card and place it in the middle of the deck. Of course, the chosen card is now on top again. Turn it over and hand it to your helper, asking him to verify his signature.

This ruse should allow you to get ready for the next move we will learn, known as the Tilt.

THE TILT

In this sleight we will apparently place a card in the middle of the deck but actually place it second from the top by creating an optical illusion.

Hold the deck face down in your left hand, as if you are getting ready for a Double-Lift but only lift one card taking about a half-inch break at the end closest to you. Angle the card leaving the other end (closest to your audience) level with the top of the deck.

Tilt the deck toward your audience and insert a card into the large break you are holding. From their viewpoint it will seem as though the card is going into the middle of the deck. In fact it goes under the top card! Make sure you practise this move – and watch your angles!

So the chosen card is now second from the top (but your audience believes it to be buried in the pack). You might want to show the face of the card just before it goes into the deck.

If you perform a Double-Lift, the chosen card will apparently be at the top once again. Now slip the top card into the middle of the deck, leaving the chosen one at the top. Hand the cards to your helper to reveal the card.

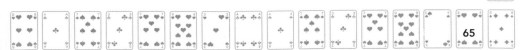

To recap:

False shuffle the chosen card to second from bottom.

Use the Shift to make it appear at the bottom.

Double-Lift and place two cards on the top.

Put the top card in the deck and reveal the chosen card.

Perform the Tilt move.

Double-Lift to show the chosen card at the top.

Place the top card in the deck.

Hand the deck to your helper to reveal the chosen card at the top again.

Phew!

Final Thoughts

There is a lot of work to be done in a trick like this, but believe me you will be rewarded for your efforts. Indeed, if you look at a lot of ambitious card routines you will find that some have many more phases than this one does. Some even repeat the same moves again and again.

In my opinion, however, such routines are dangerous because they can become very boring, and run the risk of exposing the methods through repetition. The only time such tricks work is when an experienced magician, who can counteract these sorts of problems with his wit and charm, performs them.

That said, do look up some of the more ambitious card routines; in them you will find new ideas to add to your own routine. And look up some other tricks that use the sleights of hand you have just learned – there are plenty out there and, let's face it, you have already done all the hard work!

What Have We Learned?

By using a different method to create a similar effect we can double the impact of our magic.

DOUBLE ENTRY
– a predictable finish to our triple-phase routine!

You will need
- A pack of cards
- The same helper
- A marker pen
- A sneaky turnover move

The Trick

Having dazzled your audience with your ability to make their chosen card continuously jump about the deck in the previous trick 'Lift Up!', you hark back to an earlier comment.

'You may recall that I controlled your behaviour a little earlier. Let's try to do that again, but in a slightly different way.'

You ponder the deck of cards in your hand for just a moment, cut the deck and place it down on the table.

'May I have our card back for just a moment please?' You take the card back, write something on its face and place it on the table next to the deck. 'I have written a small prediction on the card. Don't try to read it just yet – that would spoil our fun.'

You ask your helper to insert the card into one end of the deck, face down, and to leave it sticking out about half way.

'You could have placed your card anywhere in the deck between any two cards. There are literally thousands of random possibilities. But let's see what I wrote on the card.'

You turn the card so that it is face up in the deck, and your audience now sees that next to the signature you have written, 'Six of Clubs and Eight of Spades'.

You slowly turn the whole deck upside down and spread the cards to show that your helper has indeed placed the signed, chosen card directly between the Six of Clubs and the Eight of Spades.

♠♣ The Secret ♦♥

Sometimes in magic you learn a trick or a move that seems completely amazing to you as a magician, even though you know exactly how it works. One such move is the Shift move from the previous trick. I sometimes just sit with a deck in my hands, shifting cards up and down the deck watching the cards change with a wry pleasure. The move in this trick has the same effect on me.

Here's what happens. As you casually look through the cards, as if you are simply pondering their beauty, what you are actually doing is making a mental note of the top and bottom cards in the deck (in our case, the Six of Clubs and the Eight of Spades). Try not to flash the face of the deck to your audience, but don't make it seem as if you are hiding anything either.

Give the cards a false cut (*see below*) or a false shuffle (*see page 39*), making sure the top and bottom cards stay in place. Place the deck down for a moment and take back the chosen card with the signature upon it. Write the names of the top and bottom cards upon it and hand it back to your helper face down.

THE FALSE CUT

If you are clever with cards and you show this overtly, you run the risk of giving the game away as to how all your tricks are done. Yet there is, in my opinion, a need to be, if not 'showy', at least a little defter than your audience. Learning how to do a false cut can help you. Here is a false cut that retains the order of the cards, looks smooth and is easy to perform.

Hold the deck face down in your right hand, gripped between your thumb and second finger. With your left forefinger, push on the bottom left corner of the deck (at the point shown in the diagram opposite), pulling the

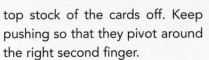

top stock of the cards off. Keep pushing so that they pivot around the right second finger.

Once the cards have spun around 180 degrees, allow them to fall into your left hand. Now place the bottom stock in your right hand and drop it down on to the table. Don't drop it smoothly – drop it from about 2cm or so. Now pick up the cards that are in your left hand with your right hand and again, drop them onto the cards you just placed on the table.

What you have done is to remove the top half of the deck, put the lower half on the table and then replace the top half exactly where it was previously. Two things sell this false cut: firstly, the dropping of the cards, and more importantly, the 180-degree swivel.

Hold the deck in your left hand and have them insert their card in the deck at any position leaving about half of the card sticking outward pointing towards your audience. Here comes the sneaky part – listen carefully!

With your right hand cut off the stock of cards above their card and turn it upside down, placing them back-to-back with the stuck-out portion of their card. Now change your grip slightly so that you are holding both that top stock of cards and their card still, in your right hand.

Turn the whole group upside down, revealing the face of the chosen card. Place the lower stock of cards that will still be in your left hand on top of (i.e. face-to-face with) their card. Place the whole deck on the table.

To your audience it will appear that you have simply turned the chosen card over in the deck, but in fact you have cut the deck halfway and repositioned the chosen card between what were previously the top and bottom cards. Practise this move a few times and you will soon be amazing yourself with your ability. All that remains now is to turn the deck over and spread out the cards to reveal your prediction – and the chosen card magically sandwiched!

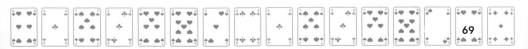

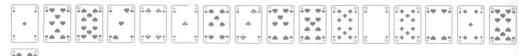

Final Thoughts

This trick makes a fitting end to our three-phase routine because it is both amazing and somewhat different from the other two tricks leading up to it. As with all our sleights of hand, this move can be used as part of a routine, to build upon other tricks or simply on its own.

When I was first shown this move it was done with a deck of cards and a business card, upon which the details of the two cards were written. In retrospect this was a good idea; if you are performing for businessmen you could borrow their cards for the trick, or you could even use your own cards. This is a great way to promote yourself and at the same time leave your audience with a tangible piece of magical memorabilia.

What Have We Learned?

We have learned that every trick or routine requires a fitting climax.

THREE GROUND RULES FOR ANY SLEIGHT OF HAND

1. It may seem obvious, but always practise your moves and sleights. Try to understand why they work and how to do them well. Do them slowly, do them quickly, stop halfway through and examine what is going on. Analyse and understand each move and sleight thoroughly.

2. Never refer to a sleight of hand while performing your tricks. Saying, 'I am going to shuffle these cards' while you are false shuffling is a sure way to draw your audience's attention to the shuffle. If they look too closely, they might see something sneaky going on.

3. Look at your audience, not your hands, cards or props. You are the centre of attention and the audience will hang on your every word. Where you look, their eyes will follow. So when you are performing your sleights, look directly at – and talk directly to – your audience. Disarm them and distract their attention away from your tricky work.

CHAPTER 6
IT'S ALL MADE UP

Have you ever heard someone referring to a person who is acting a little crazy as 'not playing with a full deck'? Well in this chapter we are going to get downright crazy – for a good part of it we won't be using a full deck of cards!

Not all card tricks require a full deck of cards. In fact, most of the cards you can buy from magic dealers these days seem to be what are known as 'packet tricks', or trick decks. These packet tricks may be made up of between three and eight cards, or they may consist of proper decks and cards that have been gimmicked in some clever way. As long as you don't fill your repertoire entirely with such tricks, they will add a touch of variety and interest to your act.

Indeed, the most famous card trick in the world is essentially a packet trick using gimmicked cards. I am, of course, referring to the 'Three-Card Trick', or 'Three-Card Monte', sometimes known as 'Find the Lady'. This trick is used all over the world as a con to fleece unsuspecting bystanders of their hard-earned cash. Most of the con men that perform this trick are very slick – I bet they could make an honest living performing real magic if they put their minds to it!

In this chapter we are going to explore some packet and full-deck tricks that will require you to make up some special cards. (The materials you will need in order to make up these cards can be found at home, or are easily available in the shops.) We'll also be reusing some of the skills we have learned so far to show how you can adapt a move or sleight and use it in a different context for a new effect.

Hopefully, by the end of this chapter you will begin to see each device – be it a gimmick, force, sleight or verbal diversion – as a separate piece in a construction set. And, after having done the

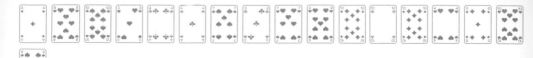

models, I'm hoping that you will have the confidence to make up some of your own. Make no mistake – the tricks in this chapter need confidence to perform. This is not because they are technically difficult, but because they are all quite easy, and hence they need the right kind of selling to really make them work. Having said that, they are all amazing tricks in their own right!

CHEESY
– a magical mouse finds the chosen card

You will need
- A pack of cards
- A special 'mouse card'
- A helper
- Some familiar moves

The Trick

Having just shown your audience one or two 'miracles', you now announce that you don't do all the magic yourself.

'I have a little magical friend, and this is his home,' you say as you pick up the card case and give it a little shake so that your audience can hear something rattling inside. You open up the case and show a playing card with a picture of a cute mouse drawn upon it. 'He doesn't have a name yet. Would you like to give him a name?' you ask. Someone offers up the name 'Albert'.

'OK – let's call him Albert,' you say. You hand the deck and Albert to your helper. 'Please shuffle the cards and make sure that Albert is well and truly lost in the deck.' You take back the cards and ask your helper to choose another card, which is also shuffled into the deck.

'Did you know you can use a deck of cards as a mousetrap?' you ask. 'I want Albert to find your card, so first let's catch him.' You riffle through the

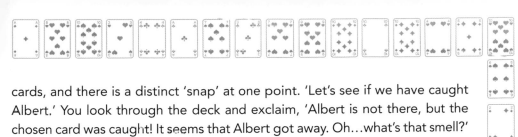

cards, and there is a distinct 'snap' at one point. 'Let's see if we have caught Albert.' You look through the deck and exclaim, 'Albert is not there, but the chosen card was caught! It seems that Albert got away. Oh…what's that smell?'

Now you sniff at the card. 'Phew! It seems like some of the cheese from the mousetrap has tainted this card. Maybe we can tempt Albert with it.'

Ask your helper now to place the card into the deck, wherever they wish, leaving one end sticking out (sound familiar?).

You turn over the cards to show that the chosen card has been placed right next to Albert – the mouse has saved the day!

The Secret

If you have already begun to work this one out for yourself, well done! If not, don't worry, but perhaps take a look back through the previous chapters and see if things become a bit clearer for you.

Essentially, this trick uses a collection of the moves and methods we have already discussed, but with one or two sleight variations. The first thing you will need is a special 'mouse card'. You will need to make this up using one of the blank-faced cards we mentioned earlier in the book (*see page 15*).

Using a permanent marker, draw a cheeky but cheerful mouse on the blank face of the card. If you are not blessed with an artistic eye, have a friend do it for you – but do ask them to make it funny rather than true to life. You will also need to trim the top edge of this card to make it into a 'short card' (*see page 15*). Leave your mouse in the card case, ready to perform.

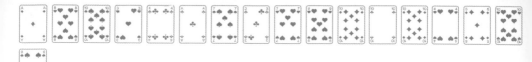

Introduce the 'mouse' and have him shuffled into the deck, then ask your helper to choose a card. Whilst your helper is looking at his card, gently riffle through the cards until you get to the break caused by the short mouse card. Casually and without a word, cut the cards here, bringing the mouse card to the top of the deck.

Place the deck on the table and ask your helper to place the chosen card on the top of the deck (and thus on top of the mouse card). Have your helper cut the deck and complete the cut, leaving the two cards in the middle of the deck. Pick up the cards and, if you wish, give them a false shuffle (*see page 39*) or a false cut (*see page 68*).

Now openly riffle through the cards, allowing them to snap loudly at the short card. This should leave the mouse card on top of the lower stock of cards and the chosen card at the face of the upper stock.

Remove the chosen card from the deck to show your audience and re-assemble the deck, switching the top and bottom halves so that the mouse card is once again on top of the deck. Now ask your helper to place the chosen card into the deck (just like in the 'Double-Entry' trick; *see page 67*) and do the same turnover move. Display the faces of the cards to show that your mouse has found the chosen card.

Final Thoughts

You might be forgiven for thinking this trick is a little twee but think again. In my experience, being too serious in card magic is not the way to win over your audience. A trick like this one can work well if there are any kids in your audience; you could even be kind and leave a youngster with your mouse card as a gift. Just make sure your trimming is neat and not too obvious.

If you do not like the mouse idea, or are unable to purchase blank cards, just draw any creature or device you wish on the card. Another simple solution would be to just use a Joker card.

What Have We Learned?

Once again, wit and charm are invaluable tools in wooing your audience.

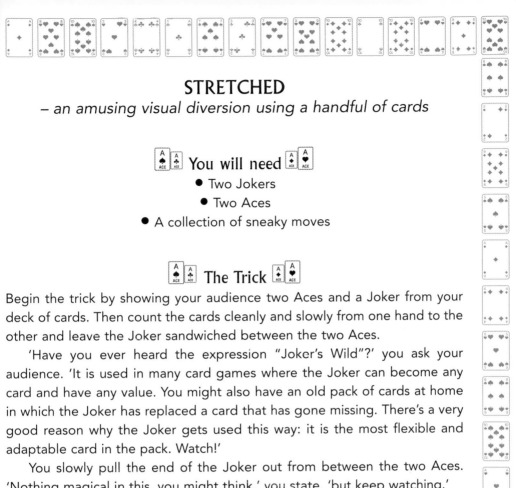

STRETCHED
– an amusing visual diversion using a handful of cards

You will need
- Two Jokers
- Two Aces
- A collection of sneaky moves

The Trick

Begin the trick by showing your audience two Aces and a Joker from your deck of cards. Then count the cards cleanly and slowly from one hand to the other and leave the Joker sandwiched between the two Aces.

'Have you ever heard the expression "Joker's Wild"?' you ask your audience. 'It is used in many card games where the Joker can become any card and have any value. You might also have an old pack of cards at home in which the Joker has replaced a card that has gone missing. There's a very good reason why the Joker gets used this way: it is the most flexible and adaptable card in the pack. Watch!'

You slowly pull the end of the Joker out from between the two Aces. 'Nothing magical in this, you might think,' you state, 'but keep watching.'

You also slowly pull the other end of the Joker from the other side of the Aces – stretching it to nearly double its length!

Just as slowly, you squeeze the two ends together and the Joker shrinks back to its normal size. You show all three cards again – and take your bow.

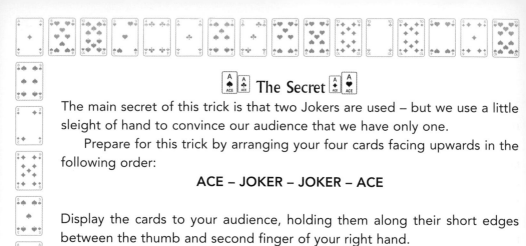

♠ ♥ The Secret ♣ ♦

The main secret of this trick is that two Jokers are used – but we use a little sleight of hand to convince our audience that we have only one.

Prepare for this trick by arranging your four cards facing upwards in the following order:

ACE – JOKER – JOKER – ACE

Display the cards to your audience, holding them along their short edges between the thumb and second finger of your right hand.

With the fingers of your left hand, draw off the bottom Ace and allow it to fall into the palm of your left hand. Now with the thumb of your left hand, draw off the top Ace, allowing it to fall onto the other Ace in your left hand. (It will help here if you apply a little inward pressure on the two Jokers in your right hand with your thumb and forefinger.) Don't bend the cards too much, but practise holding the two of them so that it looks as though there is only one card.

Use the two Jokers to flip over the top Ace so that it lies face to face with the other Ace. Now slip the two Jokers between the Aces and square all four cards up, holding them in your left hand.

To recap, in your left hand you should have (from top to bottom): a face down Ace, two face-up Jokers and a face-up Ace.

With your right hand slowly draw down the top Ace, exposing a centimetre or so of the top Joker. Again, with your right hand, push this Joker upwards so that it extends out from the packet by about half of its length.

Now push the top Ace slightly up – this will expose a part of the lower Joker. Pull the lower Joker downwards with your right hand, creating the illusion that the card has been stretched. Turn your left hand back and forth so that the audience can see all sides of the cards – this will help to sell the effect.

Now slowly and with a little drama, push the two ends of the Jokers back into place. Take the cards back between your right thumb and second finger. Draw off the upper Ace into your left hand and use the three cards in your right hand to flip it over. Draw off the bottom Ace so that it lies on top of the other one and casually slide the two Jokers as one between the two Aces.

Place the cards on top of the deck, which you can now shuffle in preparation for your next miracle.

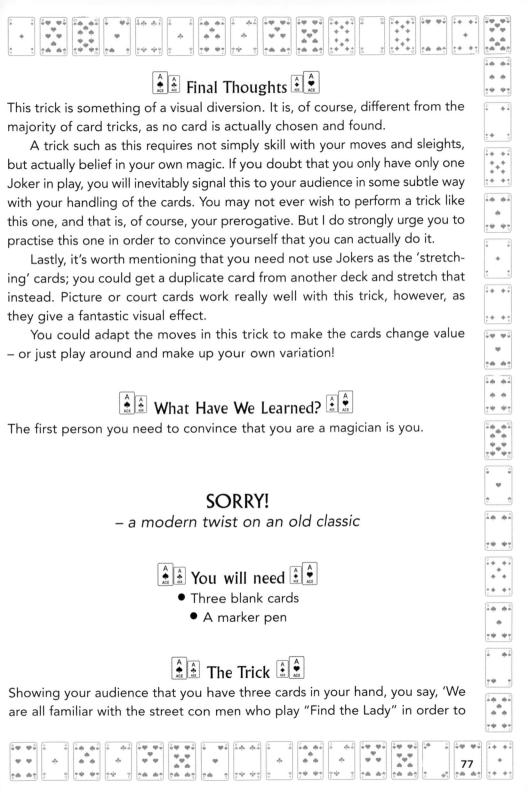

Final Thoughts

This trick is something of a visual diversion. It is, of course, different from the majority of card tricks, as no card is actually chosen and found.

A trick such as this requires not simply skill with your moves and sleights, but actually belief in your own magic. If you doubt that you only have only one Joker in play, you will inevitably signal this to your audience in some subtle way with your handling of the cards. You may not ever wish to perform a trick like this one, and that is, of course, your prerogative. But I do strongly urge you to practise this one in order to convince yourself that you can actually do it.

Lastly, it's worth mentioning that you need not use Jokers as the 'stretching' cards; you could get a duplicate card from another deck and stretch that instead. Picture or court cards work really well with this trick, however, as they give a fantastic visual effect.

You could adapt the moves in this trick to make the cards change value – or just play around and make up your own variation!

What Have We Learned?

The first person you need to convince that you are a magician is you.

SORRY!
– a modern twist on an old classic

You will need

- Three blank cards
  - A marker pen

The Trick

Showing your audience that you have three cards in your hand, you say, 'We are all familiar with the street con men who play "Find the Lady" in order to

take your money using their card skills. Well, today I am going to give you a lesson in how to win such a challenge. I will do so by showing you how to keep track of all the cards!'

You count three cards from one hand to the other, showing the backs of the cards. 'Can you see these three cards?' you ask. Your audience replies in the affirmative.

You show the faces of all three cards, and again your audience confirms that they can see all three cards. 'That's very good. We do indeed have three "Yes" cards: one on the bottom, one in the middle and one on the top. You have passed the first test,' you say as you show the cards one at a time.

'Do you think you can keep your eyes on these three cards for me?' Again, your audience answer yes. You look down at the cards. 'Oh dear – you failed to keep an eye on these cards. These are all "No" cards!'

Indeed, the three cards all now show the word 'No'. You show them to your audience. 'Would you like a second chance? Can you keep your eyes on the "No" cards for me now?' Once again your audience agrees, but you look down at the cards and are once again crestfallen.

'Oh dear,' you exclaim. 'They've gone too! Sorry, but I wouldn't take on a card man if I were you.' You show your audience that all three cards have the word 'Sorry' written upon them.

The Secret

The secret behind this trick is a series of sleights and moves designed to show the cards all to be 'Yes', then all to be 'No' and finally 'Sorry' – but what sells the effect is the amusing story you tell. To learn this trick first re-read the story and then play with each move in turn and see how they create the effect of all the cards being the same. Finally re-read the story and piece it together move by move. You'll not only benefit from knowing this trick but will be set to use these sleights in others too!

This trick employs three sleights, but they are all easy – and you already know one of them. The first is the Double-Lift, the second is a type of Double Move and the last is a Flourish move that shows all the cards as the same.

Obviously, the trick uses just three cards; make these up using blank cards and a marker pen. On one of the cards write 'Yes', on one write 'No' and on the last one write 'Sorry'.

Start off by holding the cards face down in your right hand – you've guessed it, between your thumb and second finger. Make sure that the 'Yes' card is on top, followed by the 'Sorry' card and then the 'No' card.

Count the cards into your left hand starting from the top, one at a time,

showing only the backs of the cards. In doing this you will, of course, reverse the order of the cards.

Now we are going to seem to show that the faces of all three cards are the same; however, we will actually show one card three times. We will do this using a move called the 'Flushtration Count'.

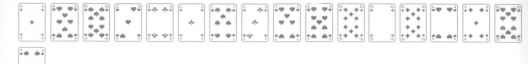

Hold the cards in your right hand, between your thumb and second finger, with the card backs towards your audience. Casually flash the face of the bottom card to your audience and turn the card face down again. Draw the top card off the packet using your left thumb, allowing it to fall into the palm of your left hand. You have now shown the front card but taken away the back one.

Repeat the move again, showing the face (of the same card) and drawing the top card onto the card in your left hand. Finally, show the face of the final card and place it into your left hand below the other two cards. Your audience will have seen three 'Yes' cards – or so they will think.

Now in your left hand you will have the 'Sorry' card on top, followed by the 'No' card with the 'Yes' card on the bottom.

Don't forget that count – you'll be using it again in a moment.

But now we need to learn another move: we are going to display the faces of the cards as all being 'Yes' one more time. Show the face of the 'Yes' card and turn the cards back downwards. Holding the cards in your left hand, pull the top card downwards about 2cm using your right hand fingers. Next push the top and middle cards back upwards and together until the top and bottom cards are aligned along the bottom edge. Use your right thumb as a stop.

Now grab the top and bottom cards with the fingers of your right hand and draw them out as one. Turn them over to show that the top card is also a 'Yes' card, and then lay them back face down on top of the bottom card.

Spread all three cards out and pull out the middle card (which is now the 'Yes' card) to show that this card is also 'Yes'. You have just shown all three cards to be 'Yes' cards in two different ways!

The order of the cards should now be (from top to bottom): 'Sorry', 'Yes' and 'No'. Perform the Flushtration Count again, followed by the moves above, to show that all three cards are now 'No' cards. Finally, perform a Flushtration Count once again to show all three cards as saying 'Sorry'!

Final Thoughts

The two sleights you have just learned are not very difficult, but they do need some thought and practice to make sure you understand what is going on when.

Practise the moves by doing them one after the other, working on your

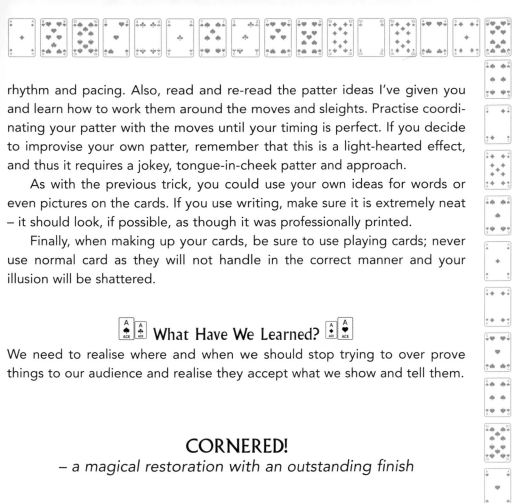

rhythm and pacing. Also, read and re-read the patter ideas I've given you and learn how to work them around the moves and sleights. Practise coordinating your patter with the moves until your timing is perfect. If you decide to improvise your own patter, remember that this is a light-hearted effect, and thus it requires a jokey, tongue-in-cheek patter and approach.

As with the previous trick, you could use your own ideas for words or even pictures on the cards. If you use writing, make sure it is extremely neat – it should look, if possible, as though it was professionally printed.

Finally, when making up your cards, be sure to use playing cards; never use normal card as they will not handle in the correct manner and your illusion will be shattered.

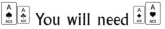 What Have We Learned?

We need to realise where and when we should stop trying to over prove things to our audience and realise they accept what we show and tell them.

CORNERED!
– a magical restoration with an outstanding finish

You will need
- A pack of cards
- A helper
- A specially prepared corner card
- An ashtray
- Some matches

The Trick

Holding your deck in your right hand, have your helper yell 'stop!' whilst you riffle through the cards. Explain to your audience that the card you've

stopped at will be the chosen card. 'I would like to do something a little bit different for this trick,' you say as you lift the chosen card from the deck.

'Normally I don't get to see the chosen card, but for this trick I want everyone, including myself, to see it plain as day. And to make sure we all recognise the card when we see it again, I will mark it so that it looks completely unique.'

Your audience gasps as you tear the chosen Five of Spades into quarters. 'Now we can't possibly mistake that for another card. Here, please keep hold of this corner as a small memento.' You hand your helper one section of the card to look after.

Now you scrunch up the remaining pieces of card, place them in an ashtray and proceed to set fire to them. As the pieces begin to smoulder and burn, you tell a ghostly tale of a witch who was burned at the stake, but managed to survive using black magic. Once the card has almost burned away, you hold the deck in the plume of smoke that is rising from the ashtray.

'Behold, the witch is unharmed!' you exclaim as you flick the side of the deck. A single card now protrudes from the deck as if by magic.

You slowly remove it and show its face – it is the Five of Spades. But surely this must be another Five of Spades, as everyone has seen the chosen one burn away... but then your audience notices this Five of Spades has a missing corner.

'Perhaps you would like to compare your corner with the card from the deck...?' you ask your helper. He offers up the corner you gave him to keep and places it next to the cornerless card – incredibly it is a perfect match!

The Secret

There are three principle secrets to this trick: a force, a duplicate card and a sleight of hand.

Prepare for this trick by getting hold of a duplicate card from a second identical deck. Tear off the top left-hand quarter of the card – one of the corners with the index on it. Place the torn corner in your jacket pocket.

You now have a pair of almost identical cards – a whole card and a duplicate with one corner missing. Now cut the deck in the middle and place

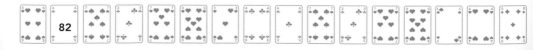

your whole card on top of the lower stock. Place the torn duplicate card on top of this card, and then place the top half of the deck on top of the torn duplicate card.

We have already seen how a short card causes a stop as we riffle through a deck – and how we can use this to force a card. Well, think about the torn card in the deck as a force card, as it is naturally short at one corner.

Now that you know how to force the card, hold the deck in your right hand and riffle your thumb along it. Ask your helper to call 'stop!' whenever he wishes; with some practice, you will learn how to stop the deck when he does so. You can then hand your helper the next card (i.e. the whole card) as the chosen card.

Close the deck again, leaving the torn card in the middle, and place it down on the table. Be careful not to flash the torn card during the selection.

Whilst your helper is examining the chosen card, casually drop your hand into your pocket and grab the loose corner. Hold it between the middle phalanx of your finger and the palm of your hand. Take back the chosen card and hold it in your hand on top of the corner. Now tear it into quarters. Make sure you do not tear the odd corner again whilst doing this.

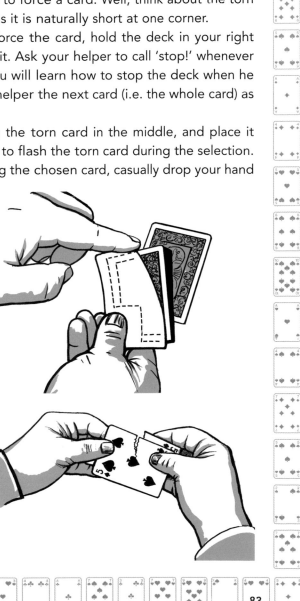

Ask your helper to hold out his hand and turn your hand (the one with the pieces of card in it) face down. Push off the top piece (this is the odd corner you had hidden in your pocket) and let it slip into his hand.

Scrunch up the remaining pieces of torn card so that they cannot be closely examined

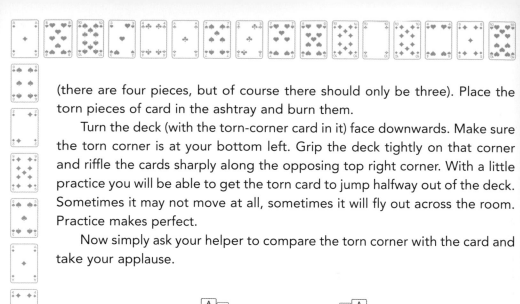

(there are four pieces, but of course there should only be three). Place the torn pieces of card in the ashtray and burn them.

Turn the deck (with the torn-corner card in it) face downwards. Make sure the torn corner is at your bottom left. Grip the deck tightly on that corner and riffle the cards sharply along the opposing top right corner. With a little practice you will be able to get the torn card to jump halfway out of the deck. Sometimes it may not move at all, sometimes it will fly out across the room. Practice makes perfect.

Now simply ask your helper to compare the torn corner with the card and take your applause.

Final Thoughts

The first thing I need to state is rather obvious: always be extremely careful when using fire during a trick! It goes without saying that you should not perform this trick anywhere near flammable material, or where children are present. A card will not burn for long, however, so the risk of danger is relatively minimal.

Another tip is to make sure that the card has mostly burned away before you produce the duplicate again or you'll give the game away!

If you are worried about using fire in this trick, you could try other ways of making your pieces vanish. One good substitute is a device called a 'Devil's Hanky'; a rather scary name for an innocent, double-thickness hanky with a secret compartment into which props can vanish. You can buy these hankies at most magic shops.

What Have We Learned?

Even an astounding visual trick can benefit from a good use of dramatics.

CHAPTER 7
KILLER 'KARDS'

As we have gone through this book together we have learned many lessons, and at this point I advise you to go back and read the 'What Have We Learned?' sections again. If I had to sum up all these points, I would say that it is your personality and desire to entertain that should govern the time, place and content of your performance.

Anytime you see a great trick performed by another magician, try to work out how it was done. Try looking the trick up in a book, or ask about it at a magic shop. Once you've discovered how the trick was done, spend lots of time playing around with it and learning it in detail.

After you have mastered the trick in question, you will have a big decision to make: shall I use it or lose it?

In showbiz one should always go out with a bang, and thus in this final chapter we will learn how to perform three great tricks, along with a rather smart card flourish to round things off. These tricks will not require any great skill, but they will require your personality to sell them. We'll finish off with a neat little card flourish that you can adapt as another false shuffle.

Enjoy!

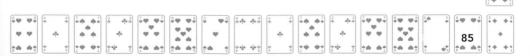

YOUR CHOICE
– the fairest and freest prediction of a single card possible!

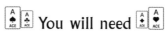 **You will need**
- A pack of cards
- Three duplicate cards from another pack
- A helper
- A wallet with a credit-card pocket
- Scissors or a box cutter
- A marker pen
- A short card
- Some marked cards

The Trick

Begin the trick by laying your deck of cards and your wallet onto the table.

'I often see in my mind how events will turn out. Just yesterday I saw myself in a room much like this one, performing magic, and a certain card was chosen. I took that one card from another deck and placed it in my wallet as a kind of prediction.'

You flip open your wallet to show that there is indeed a card stowed safely away in it but do not show your audience what the card is. Shuffle the cards and hand them to your helper to cut. Now take them back and mix them up a bit more, then hand them back to your helper. Look him squarely in the eye.

'I want this to be all about your choice,' you say. 'Please deal a pile of cards onto the table, face downwards. The exact number of cards is up to you, but around a half to a third of the deck would be ideal.'

After he has counted off the cards, you look at him again. 'Now you chose these cards of your own volition, yes?' He nods.

'Good, now deal the cards into three hands, one at a time, keeping the cards face down.' He does so.

You now point to one hand and ask, 'Do you wish to eliminate or keep this hand? It's your choice.' He answers, 'Eliminate'. You now point to one of

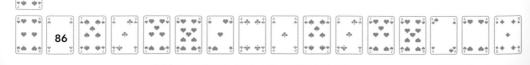

the other hands, and ask the same question. This time he answers, 'Keep'.

You point to the remaining hand and say, '…in which case I take it you wish to eliminate this hand? Now you may change your mind – again, *it is your choice.*' He confirms his choice and we are left with the second hand. You now open your wallet and remove the card you had shown earlier. You lay it, face down, next to the chosen hand.

'Please turn over the top cards on the two hands we have eliminated,' you say. 'They are the Eight of Clubs and the Two of Diamonds – both perfectly nice cards, but neither of them are your choice. Now turn over the top card on your chosen hand. The Seven of Spades – this card is *your choice!*'

You now ask him to turn over your prediction card – it is also the Seven of Spades. 'Ah, the Seven of Spades! This card is just like yours – only this time it was *my choice!*'

♠♣ The Secret ♠♥

The first items we need for this trick are three cards from another deck. These will be our 'prediction' cards, which we will keep in our wallet. Choose three different values, such as Two, Seven and Eight.

Place the three cards in your wallet. Put the Two on top of the Seven and slip the two cards into a credit-card pocket within the wallet. Put the Eight behind the Seven, but in the next pocket of your wallet.

Now retrieve the duplicates of these three cards from your deck. Trim one to be a short card. Find a marker pen the same colour as your back design, and on the other two cards make a mark near their centres by filling in an area of white. (You will have to decide exactly where to make the markings based upon the design of your cards – you are trying to make the three cards distinguishable when glancing quickly at their backs.) Mark one card in one way, the next in another and leave the short card unmarked. Do not make the marks so obvious that your audience can spot them.

Place these three cards on top of the deck with the short card right at the top. The rest of the trick is a breeze! Start the trick by casually showing the 'single' prediction card in your wallet. False shuffle the cards (*see page 39*) and cut them at will. Hand them to your helper to be cut again. Upon taking

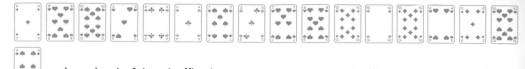

them back, false shuffle them one more time and riffle to the short card. Cut it (and the two other cards) to the top.

Hand the deck to your helper and have him deal out some of the cards. Explain that he needs to deal out no less than a third of the deck. Around 20 would be perfect, but any number above 13 will suffice. Less than a dozen can weaken the effect. Our three cards will now be at the bottom of the pile.

Have your helper deal the cards into three 'hands'. (Note that we say 'hands' rather than 'piles', as a hand implies that the cards are being dealt out to each pile in rotation.) Whether the number of cards is divisible by three or not, our three cards should now be the top cards in each hand.

Go through the hand elimination process, making it as fair as you can. Allow your helper to change his mind if he wishes – you have no need to worry as you have a card for each outcome in your wallet!

Once your helper chooses his hand, glimpse the marking on the back of the top card of the hand and establish which card it is. Pick up your wallet and show the 'single' prediction card again. Now turn the wallet towards yourself and go to remove the card. All you have to do is recall the order the three cards are in – low, middle to high value from the front to back of the wallet! So it is not hard for you to get to the right card.

Grab the correct card and draw it out of the wallet with your thumb and fingers, pushing the other cards down further into the pockets, so that they are hidden. Casually flash the inside of the wallet to show that it is 'empty' and put it away in your jacket or coat pocket.

Reveal your prediction and your job is done.

Final Thoughts

A few years ago this was my favourite card trick; it was the product of a moment's inspiration, having played with the workings of some other tricks I knew. You might be surprised to learn that despite the simplicity of the trick, I actually performed it at my entrance examination to the world-famous Magic Circle (a prestigious magician's society).

Your choice of wallet is important here. While you can buy lots of nice trick wallets from magic stores, you shouldn't use one of them for this trick.

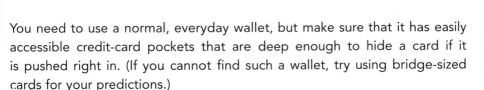

You need to use a normal, everyday wallet, but make sure that it has easily accessible credit-card pockets that are deep enough to hide a card if it is pushed right in. (If you cannot find such a wallet, try using bridge-sized cards for your predictions.)

Once you have found a wallet that is suitable, fill it with 'normal' items: bills, credit cards and a photograph of your partner. Make it look like a normal wallet and no one will suspect a thing, whereas a pristine wallet with just a card in it will arouse suspicion.

What Have We Learned?

Real magic doesn't involve pristine, shiny props – it is far more effective if your props appear to be real.

RUNAROUND!
– a revelation of the four Aces

You will need
- A pack of cards
- A helper
- A false shuffle or cut
- An optional flourish or two

The Trick

You begin the trick by saying to your audience, 'One thing that people often say to me is "I wouldn't want to play cards with you." I'll show you why they say this!' Give the deck a quick shuffle and a cut and lay it out on the table.

'Cut the deck in half for me please,' you ask your helper, 'and lay the top half of it next to the lower half. Now cut each half again, making four piles, and leave them on the table.' You look back and forth between your helper

and the cards as you slide the piles around the table, trying to decide what goes where.

'Ah – that will do nicely!' you say, apparently satisfied.

You point to one of the piles and politely instruct your helper, 'Please deal one card from the top of that pile onto each of the other piles. Now count three cards from the top of that pile to the bottom.' He does so and replaces the cards on the table.

'OK, now pick up this next pile and count three cards from top to bottom and then deal a card onto each of the piles. Now take this third pile and deal a card onto each of the other piles and count three to the bottom. Finally, take our last pile, count three to the bottom and deal one card onto each of the other piles.' Your helper completes his work and lays down the cards.

'These cards have been shuffled and randomised, and you have seen all the work done right here!' you exclaim. 'And the reason people won't play cards with me is...' You turn over the top card in each pile.

'I always know where the Aces are!' Indeed, the top card on each pile is an Ace!

The Secret

This trick really does work itself, and is truly fun to perform.

Start off with the four Aces on the top of the deck. Give the deck a false shuffle and a cut and then hand it over to your helper. Ask him to cut the deck first into two piles, and then to cut each of those piles into two, making

a total of four piles. All you have to do is to make sure you follow the original top stock of cards (the one with the Aces on top), as this is key to the trick.

Move the piles around the table as if you are making some kind of informed choice as to where they should go. Their placement is, in fact, irrelevant, but this act serves to confuse and divert your audience's attention away from what is really going on.

Go through the process of dealing the cards from the top of each pile onto the others, and then counting three from the top to the bottom and vice versa, as explained above. Make sure, of course, that the last pile you do this with is the pile that contains your Aces.

If you stop and think for a moment, you will realise that you have dealt a card from the top of each of the three other piles onto the Aces. You then deal those three cards to the bottom of the Ace pile. Then you deal three Aces onto the tops of the other piles, leaving one Ace still atop the Ace pile.

All four piles now have an Ace on top – what could be simpler than that!

Final Thoughts

The more byplay you can build into this trick, the better it works, so try to really make a fuss about aligning the cards and moving them into place.

There is one thing to watch when performing a self-working trick like this: it is so simple the audience may just cotton on to what you've done. The solution to this is, as stated, to inject some drama into your performance.

Some magic books and DVDs contain a more involved version of this trick, with more variations on the movements. Look these up for some new ideas – or just make up your own variations.

Remember that any deviation will rely upon the simple principle of knowing where the Aces are; all you really have to do is to keep track of them and move the right cards around until they are left on top!

What Have We Learned?

In a nutshell, a sharp eye can be just as effective as a quick hand.

ABSOLUTE ABSURDITY
– a most absurd prediction of your helper's choice

You will need
- A pack of cards
- A helper

The Trick

You hand a pack of cards to your helper and ask him to shuffle it thoroughly.

'I want you to lay the cards on the table and to cut off a random quantity of cards. I will do the same after you have done so.'

You both take a section of cards from the deck, leaving the remainder on the table. 'Now I want you to count your cards. I will count mine too, and, for the moment, no one else can know how many cards we each have. So lets turn our backs as we count.'

Both of you count your cards, then turn around and face each other again.

'I am going to predict your actions in relation to mine,' you say. 'You took a random number of cards – is that correct? You see I believe that I have the same number of cards as you, with 3 to spare plus enough to give you 18 cards in total. Now count your cards with me onto the table.'

Your helper counts, '1, 2, 3, 4, 5, 6, 7, 8, 9, 10, 11.' He stops there, as he has run out of cards.

'Like I said, I have 3 spare,' you say. You count three cards off to one side. 'And enough to give you 18 cards in total!' You carry on counting the remainder of your cards onto his cards, '...12, 13, 14, 15, 16, 17 and 18!'

Your prediction was correct. Your helper walks away, scratching his head.

The Secret

Before I explain how to do this trick, please make me one promise: that you will not discount it! Yes, it is absurdly simple and, in many ways, absurdly obvious. But that, I think, is its natural beauty. In fact, there isn't a trick here

THE CHARLIER CUT

Despite what I said earlier about not wishing to appear too flashy when doing card tricks, the occasional flourish – particularly when we are doing a trick such as the one above, which shows our mastery of the four Aces – has its rightful place.

When I was a child I tried for years to get this move right; I cracked it when I was about 12 years old. The reason it took so long for me to learn was that my hands were too small. So, just to show off, we are going to cut the deck using one hand only!

Hold the deck in your right hand at the tips of your fingers and thumb (*see illustrations below*). Your fingers should be along one long edge, with your thumb along the other long edge. Your index finger, however, must not make contact with the cards – yet.

If you slightly tilt your thumb upwards it will lose contact with the lower cards of the deck, and they will fall at an angle into the palm of your hand. Now, with your index finger, push the top edge of these fallen cards towards your thumb. They will slowly push the remaining cards upwards, releasing those cards from your thumb. Push further still until the lower cards clear the upper cards. The upper cards will now fall behind the lower cards. You have cut the deck with one hand!

This manoeuvre does require some practice. A good tip is to separate the deck into two halves and wrap an elastic band around each. This way you can get used to moving the card stocks around without them flying all over the floor.

Once you have mastered the Charlier cut, try gathering the cards into your left hand whilst retaining the break between the two halves. By then performing a double undercut you will have a flashy flourish false cut!

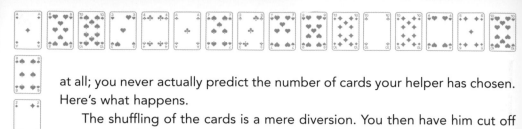

at all; you never actually predict the number of cards your helper has chosen. Here's what happens.

The shuffling of the cards is a mere diversion. You then have him cut off some cards from the deck. Try and see how large his selection is. All you need do now is to take a much larger pile yourself!

You each count your cards. Let's say, as in the example above, that you have selected 21 cards in total. Before you ask how many cards your helper has, you pronounce, 'I have the same number of cards as you do, with 3 to spare plus enough to give you 18 cards in total.'

Let's analyse this statement. You have 21 cards; that's 18 plus 3. That is all you have stated, but because you imply that the first 11 of those cards are his, the whole quantity you seem to have predicted apparently belongs to him.

So you now count your cards out together, counting aloud as you go. In our example he will stop counting at 11, whereupon you will count 3 cards off to one side (your '3 spare') and then continue counting the balance of your cards onto his pile until he has 18 cards in total.

Each time you do this trick you will need to think on your feet and chose a different number of 'spare' cards – the actual number is, of course, irrelevant – it just has to allow you to count out the correct number of cards to give your helper 18 cards in total.

Final Thoughts

This trick holds a special place in my heart. I read about it some time ago in a dusty old book and loved it immediately, but I didn't believe I could pull it off until I actually performed it. I then showed it to one of my very best magician friends – a most excellent card magician – and he was completely stumped. This is quite amazing as if you think about it there isn't even a trick here!

One last thing to note is that you don't need to use cards to perform this trick; you can use coins, matches or even peanuts – whatever lies to hand!

What Have We Learned?

We have learned here that the magic really happens in our audience's mind!

FURTHER READING

The following is a list of titles that will help you further your knowledge of card magic.

GENERAL CARD MAGIC BOOKS

Karl Fulves, *Self Working Card Tricks*, Dover Publications

Hugard, Crimmins & Bailey, *Encyclopedia of Card Tricks*, Foulsham

Hugard, Braue & Bailey, *The Royal Road to Card Magic*, Foulsham

Mark Wilson, *Complete Course in Magic*, Running Press

OTHER BOOKS BY MARC LEMEZMA:
Marc Lemezma's Mind Tricks, New Holland

Mind Magic, New Holland

Every Magic Secret in the World Revealed!, New Holland

The Complete Fortune Teller, New Holland

Magic Tricks, Marks & Spencer (co-authored)

How to be a Mind Magician, Tobar

USEFUL ADDRESSES

Here are a few addresses of dealers in all things magic, along with some websites, magazines, clubs and societies that may be of interest. I begin with my own website, www.lemezma.com.

MAGIC DEALERS
Alakazam Magic
www.alakazam.co.uk

International Magic
www.internationalmagic.com

Hank Lee's Magic Factory
www.hanklee.com

MAGIC MAGAZINES
Magic Week
www.magicweek.com
Online newsletter updated weekly

Genii Magazine
www.geniimagazine.com

MAGIC CLUBS AND SOCIETIES
There are literally thousands of magic clubs and societies around the world. Here are some details from two of the most prominent, which will no doubt help you locate some magical friends local to you!

The Magic Circle
www.themagiccircle.co.uk

The International Brotherhood of Magicians
www.magician.org

AUTHOR BIOGRAPHY AND NOTE

Marc Lemezma is a professional Magician, Presenter and After-Dinner Speaker from the United Kingdom. He has performed across the world for countless thousands of people including many celebrities, politicians and even Her Majesty the Queen. A prolific writer on Magic, all things mystical and business communications, Marc already has several books and many articles published in print and on-line in several languages.

© David Hebditch, Portland Studios Photography

I can't believe I have finished my seventh book in just five years! I would need another seven books to fully list all those to whom I owe a debt of gratitude. For you see there is little new in Magic and all magicians everywhere contribute to the heritage of our art form in some way or other.

Thus to all the magicians in the World – whether you have inspired me with your greatness or unwittingly educated me through your own errors – THANK YOU!

I must also offer my continued thanks to Julia and the whole team at New Holland who have guided me through this tricky process one more time.

Finally to Emma, who continues to fill my heart with inspiration and passion.

Marc Lemezma